Buy-outs

Published by
Euromoney Books
and
Orion Publishing

Published by
Euromoney Books PLC
Nestor House, Playhouse Yard
London EC4V 5EX

Acknowledgements

Buy-outs has grown from the Euromoney book
The Management Buy-Out Manual published in
1993 and edited by Garry Sharp.

The publishers would like to thank the following
for their assistance in producing this book:

Authors
David Barraclough (Midland Bank)

David Bellringer (Binder Hamlyn)

Lorraine Boyle (Corporate Risk)

Patrick Dunne (3i)

Geoffrey Green (Ashurst Morris Crisp)

Gordon Maclean (3i)

Martin Makey (ECI Ventures)

Lindsey Page (Binder Hamlyn)

Peter Stowell (Barclays Bank)

Caroline Corby, Chris Masterson and Roger Heath (Montagu Private Equity)

Editor
Vince O'Brien, Director, Montagu Private Equity

Sub-Editor
Alan Foster

Designers
RDDA and Response Advertising

Typesetters
PW Reprosharp

Printers
Redwood Books Limited

Contents

Foreword

After a year in which institutional investors around the world committed more than £1 billion of new capital to United Kingdom venture capital institutions, it can, with some certainty, be said that the management buy-out industry is in good health. The British Venture Capital Association, the representative body for the UK's venture capital industry, lists well over a hundred institutions willing to provide venture capital to successful entrepreneurs. Management buy-outs and various derivations of management buy-outs continue to absorb the lion's share of this capital and activity in the United Kingdom in 1994 has been at its highest level since the late 1980s.

Management buy-outs in the United Kingdom have a relatively short history and can be traced back to the late 1970s. The concept really took off in the course of the recession in the early 1980s when many large groups were looking to sell off non-core subsidiaries in order to raise cash. After a period of rapid growth buy-outs then peaked in the late 1980s. Despite some slight fall in numbers of deals in recent years they have remained a significant proportion of all merger and acquisition activity in the UK and have recovered significantly in 1994. This book is deliberately targeted at United Kingdom management teams. However, activity on the continent continues to increase and there are large and active MBO markets in most Continental European countries.

Many managers have made a big success of buying the business they used to manage and with the development of the industry in the UK we have seen a number of new concepts:

– Increasingly in the 1980s we have witnessed the growth of the management buy-in ('MBI') whereby a team of managers from outside the company buy the business having convinced their financial backers that they can add value through their management expertise.

- The growth in MBIs in recent years has been substantial, and inevitably a hybrid of the two types of deal has developed. The MBIO or BIMBO is a transaction which combines internal and external managements' expertise to acquire the business. Whilst the term is relatively new, the concept of beefing up the existing management team with one, two or more outsiders is one that has been used by practitioners for some time.
- The MEBO is a buy-out which involves management and employees in acquiring the business and the growth of this concept, notable in such buy-outs as those of Clydeport and the recently privatised London Bus companies, has introduced the concept of the buy-out to a vast number of employees in the United Kingdom. They have been given first hand experience of participating in the share ownership of their company and benefiting directly from the success of the business.
- Another increasingly popular term is the VIMBO, the vendor initiated management buy-out. As the private equity institutions become more adept at acquiring businesses, so vendors are increasingly using the buy-out backed by a financial institution as a good tool for disposing of subsidiaries which are either unwanted or no longer fit in with the group's strategy.

Successful MBOs have been carried out in every type of industry from engineering and manufacturing to retailing, leisure and financial services. There is now no limit to the size of deal that can be achieved in the UK as is evidenced by such deals as the £405 million management buy-out of Gardner Merchant. Given a high quality management team and the right price, deals are being done.

The aim and purpose of this book are set out in Chapter One. In brief the book is intended to be used as a manual for the management team wishing to do a buy-out or for the general reader or practitioner. It can be read either as a continuous text or each chapter used as a point of reference. The contributors range across the whole spectrum of the industry and my thanks go to them for their co-operation. They are all practitioners with a wealth of experience in arranging and advising on management buy-outs and their views, taken together, reflect the combined expertise of the largest market for management buy-outs in Europe.

If you are an entrepreneur and you are looking to do a management buy-out, I hope that you will find the next hundred pages or so useful both as a starting point and as an aide-memoire in the course of doing your deal. Of course, the book can only give guidance and you are advised to take professional advice at all stages. The buy-out process is a testing one. It is usually exciting, often exhilarating and at times, frustrating. However, I believe that you will find the experience rewarding. Having been through the process on many occasions with many successful management teams I would advise you to persevere and never give up the fight. As a famous boxing promoter once said, 'You must believe the unbelievable and snatch the possible out of the impossible'.

Good Luck.

Introduction

The buy-out process – 'Never Again!'

One day, the Managing Director of ABC Limited, a manufacturing subsidiary of the Corporation Group plc, hears that his company may be up for sale and that he and his management team might be offered the opportunity to buy the company. The news sparks much excitement. He now considers what to do next and a number of questions flash through his mind. What do I do? Who do I talk to? How much will it cost? Where do I get the money? How do I know what to pay? Who will back me? Which bank? Which lawyers? How long will it take?

Several months later, the Managing Director and his team are signing a sale and purchase agreement. They have finally bought their company. They have been backed by financial institutions willing to stake millions in equity and loan finance on their future performance. They now own a significant stake in the company. They expect it to prosper. Indeed it had better prosper because they have put their own money into it!

They have worked long hours, often outside normal office time. They have prepared business plans, selected advisors and backers, and have negotiated a price with the vendor or parent group. They have run projections through a computer model, explained to potential backers how their business works for the umpteenth time and have dealt with weeks of being investigated by reporting accountants. They have analysed and re-analysed the marketplace to satisfy a team of reporting consultants and re-run those projections again. They have attended seemingly interminable meetings with the lawyers, responded to doubts expressed about the quality of some members of the team and have explained why the latest month's results differ to budget..... all whilst trying to keep the business running smoothly!

No wonder the parting words from the successful team are often "Never again!" As they depart to see their families for the first time in weeks, they will look back on a process which most of them are likely to experience only once in their lives. A process that most find exhilarating, frustrating and very often exhausting. In fact, this is only the beginning of the next stage, that of making the deal work by achieving all their forecasts and giving its backers the returns they want. However, for the moment, they can sit back and ponder the highs and lows of the previous months.

The Purpose of this Book

The purpose of this book is to prepare the management team or the general reader for the process described and to give them some advance notice of what to expect once they have decided to embark on an MBO. The book seeks to identify the key considerations which may arise during this once-in-a-lifetime experience and to give the management team an appreciation of some of the principles involved.

The book is a manual for the management team but it cannot give all the answers. It seeks to establish a comprehensive set of principles across a selection of key areas but it does not set out rules and it avoids checklists as far as possible. Indeed, the management team will find that virtually every advisor they meet will happily supply them with checklists. They will see checklists of what should go in to a Business Plan, into an offer letter, what to look for in a funding letter, what personal tax points they should be aware of, what should go in the Memorandum and Articles, what to watch for in the shareholders agreement.

The book is designed to be read through quickly, say at the start of the deal, but is broken into chapters which can also stand alone, thereby providing a quick point of reference on any particular area of concern. It is, in effect, an introduction for the manager as well as a descriptive outline of the MBO process.

How the Topic is Covered

In this first chapter, we set the scene by introducing some general issues such as what factors make for a successful buy-out and a brief commentary on MBO's in Europe. We then cover each key area in individual chapters:-

– Chapter Two takes the reader through **the steps involved** in doing a buy-out and covers choosing advisers, preparing business plans, choosing backers and negotiating with the vendor.
– In Chapter Three the principles of **structuring the transaction** are covered. This is a topic which could fill a book in itself and the text concentrates on the aspects which are common to most MBO's.

– The role of **the banker** is covered in Chapter Four. The amount of leverage that can be accommodated in a deal is a vital ingredient for a successful MBO and it is essential for the management team to be aware of the means by which the provider of debt assesses a proposal.

- Chapter Five outlines the **due diligence** process. Many buy-outs founder because the golden future being projected for the business in management's business plan fails to stand up to critical review. It is well worth noting the principles involved in this area and being aware of the need to satisfy the most critical of investigations before the backers will part with their money.
- In Chapter Six we look at the main **tax considerations** involved in an MBO. In this area there is of course no substitute for good advice and every deal is likely to have its own particular nuance. However, there are some general principles which can be applied to most situations, and with the increasing popularity of employee buy-outs, the question of (whether and) how best to bring in the employees is worth considering early.
- Chapter Seven covers the **role of the lawyer**. It deals with the documentation likely to be necessary on a deal and also illustrates how a pro-active lawyer can often provide a great deal of added value to the buy-out process.
- In Chapter Eight we cover the **insurance aspects** of a MBO. This is an area very often neglected until the later stage of a deal – often with perilous consequences.
- Chapter Nine also looks at an area which often is not considered until the deal process is underway – **the period after a buy-out**. This is the time when the work to make the deal a success begins – projections have to be achieved and returns obtained.
- Chapters Ten and Eleven then provide some statistical analysis of the United Kingdom marketplace. Chapter Ten considers the growth of **the management buy-in** as a tool for change whilst Chapter Eleven provides some statistics covering **the larger management buy-outs**, attempting to draw some conclusions as to structures and the future for the bigger deals.

A word about Continental Europe

The book concentrates on doing deals in the United Kingdom. Whilst a thriving MBO market exists in Continental Europe, many of the principles covered will vary from country to country and a detailed consideration of how to approach a buy-out in each country is best dealt with in a separate volume.

For some years, the United Kingdom has led the field in the buy-out arena. The most recently available statistics show that there were more buy-outs in the United Kingdom in 1994 than in any other European country. (For a detailed analysis, see the Centre for Management Buy-Outs Annual Review).

Indeed, the United Kingdom throughout the 1980s has led the way for Europe and many have speculated as to why this should be so. John Singer, the former Chairman of the European Venture Capital Association, pointed out a number of technical, regulatory and cultural reasons as to why activity in the Continent was less advanced and considerably more volatile than in the United Kingdom. Among the fundamental differences are:-

- Whilst in Europe, much venture capital comes from banking institutions, in the UK the banks tend to avoid holding 100% of the equity of companies. Although the major clearing banks have thriving venture capital operations, there has, throughout the 1980's, been a growth of institutions which specialise in funding buy-outs. This has created an industry specifically geared towards promoting the buy-out concept. Indeed, the British Venture Capital Association lists more than one hundred full members providing venture capital to the United Kingdom market.
- The United Kingdom has continued to attract the great majority of institutional funding coming into Europe. In 1994 a record amount of institutional funds (over £1 billion according to most estimates) were raised to finance venture capital and the continued availability of such funds has further helped fuel the industry.

Other factors which favour the UK are the quality of exit routes, in particular the London Stock Exchange, whose existence provides a ready made means for institutions to realise their investment. Moreover the legislative environment in the UK has also tended to be more favourable to buy-outs. For example, the Companies Act in the UK provides a means for a company's assets to be used as security to raise debt for its acquisition. In most countries in Continental Europe this is a basic obstacle to MBO financing.

In addition, there are some cultural differences which John Singer has highlighted. He argues, for example, that the entrepreneurial ethos in the UK and USA encourages entrepreneurs to want to own their own businesses so that acquisition and disposal activity has become firmly embedded in the respective cultures. By contrast, the mainland of Europe has a commercial culture which encourages a heightened sense of loyalty by managers to their companies and owners. Subsidiary businesses and family businesses are not traded as frequently and there is therefore less pressure for buy-out activity.

Despite these factors, activity in Continental Europe continues to grow and the hurdles are being, and will be, surmounted in due course. Indeed after something of a false start in the 1980's more and more United Kingdom-based venture capital providers are expecting Continental Europe to become a major area of operations in the mid to late 1990s and beyond.

What makes for a good buy-out?

Before addressing the process of doing a deal, let us consider the factors that make for a successful buy-out. Perhaps the top five ingredients are the following:-

- Quality business
- Quality management
- Committed institutions
- The correct structure
- Clear exit route

All buy-outs are different and it is very rare that all of these characteristics are present in exactly the right proportions. Indeed, different institutions and different advisors would no doubt choose some other ingredients in their top five. However, the list is a fairly universal one and by considering each briefly, the manager leading a buy-out may even be able to spot ways in which his buy-out mix can be improved.

Quality business

If an institution is to be expected to commit large sums of its money to back a team, it will only do so provided the business being backed is sound. Buy-outs have been achieved across a broad spectrum of industries, from manufacturing to media, property and real estate to software and research. However, in all cases there has to be a belief in the quality of the underlying business. A backer will carry out any amount of theoretical analysis but, in the simplest terms, he will want to satisfy himself that the company has:-

– secure market position
– good predictable cash flows
– real growth potential
– ability to avoid or cope with fluctuations in the business cycle
– good financial systems and controls
– sound customer base
– good track record

Many potential deals are rejected because they depend upon some change in the nature of the business. Institutions are wary of the Managing Director who says: 'Our margins are currently being squeezed and we've lost a few customers, but in the first year after the buy-out we're moving into a new product line which we are sure will win us a lot more high-margin business'. Whilst this is a fine goal with which to inspire salesmen and to set targets it is unlikely to convince an investment banker to part with his cash.

The effect of business cycles is also worthy of note. Buy-outs depend upon good, safe, predictable cash flows but in many industries, such as say food production, the cycles are severe. However, this does not necessarily make a deal unworkable and, as Chapter Three will show, a deal can be structured so as to take unusual business cycles into account, provided of course that the underlying business is sound.

A proven track record of achievement is also important, as is a market position which will enable the company to achieve its growth potential. The returns to all parties rest upon the management team's ability to increase the value of the business and this is unlikely to be possible unless the business has the ability to maintain or capture market share.

Quality Management

There are many views on what makes a good management team and whether a team has the correct mix of talents is necessarily a subjective opinion. However, many financial backers would agree that having the right team is the first and main ingredient in the buy-out recipe. Indeed, it is anecdotal in the venture capital industry that many would-be backers, on receipt of a business plan, will read the personal biographies of the team before reading anything else and, most likely, will form their initial views on the strength of them. If the team looks right, then the chances are that the business they want to buy will be right too. If the team looks weak on paper, the buy-out in the form anticipated is already starting at a disadvantage.

Once again, there are no rules as to what makes a backable team. Usually, however, the backers will expect to see at least the following:-

– a recognised and motivated leader
– the right balance of skills
– good records of achievement for each
– a well thought-out and realistic business plan.
– a good grasp of the process involved
– no signs of divisions in the team

The last point is critical. All the team will need to be committed to give the time and effort necessary to complete the deal. If there is any suggestion that one or more of the team is not committed to working to the common goal, either through a lack of motivation or a personality clash, this needs to be dealt with quickly. Similarly if there is an obvious weak link in the team it is best to address the matter up front – if the management team do not deal with this the backers surely will.

Committed Institutions

Some buy-outs fail because the institutional backers prove not to be as enthusiastic about the business as may have originally seemed. Committed backers are essential and, if there are real doubts about whether the institution will finally commit to the deal, it is worth raising them straight away. These doubts might manifest themselves in a reluctance on the part of the institution to give a real indication of the extent of its financial support, or perhaps an over-optimistic offer for the business. The team and its advisors should be wary of the institution which bids high to win the mandate for a deal and then spends months chipping away at the terms so as to get its commitment down to where it should have been in the first place.

Committed backers are also essential when the deal has been completed. The institution has backed the management team to run the business in accordance with a plan. But no plan can ever anticipate all eventualities. Something may go wrong, say the loss of a large contract, or an opportunity may arise, such as the chance of making a useful acquisition, which was not anticipated at the time of the buy-out. Results may be behind plan perhaps because a trend in the market was misread. In such cases, the management team will usually look for support from the institutional backer and will not want an institution that panics at the first sight of trouble.

The Correct Structure

The perfect deal will have the perfect structure. The right price will have been paid. The financial commitment from the management team will be just right for them, the company will achieve all of its forecasts, bank debt will repaid on schedule and the equity players will get their required return.

Of course, real life is never like this and the structure will never be perfect for everybody. However, the message for the management is : ignore the structure at your peril. A badly structured deal will cause a great deal of heartache. It is likely to result in ill-feeling from the parties who suffer most. Even when the business performs as expected, it can seriously detract from the success of the buy-out.

As Chapter Three shows, there is no typical deal structure. However, the industry can point to plenty of examples of deals which have been badly structured. Other than simply paying too much for the business the chief problems encountered are:-

– over-optimistic projections
– ratchets that don't work
– covenants that are drawn too tightly
– over-ambitious bank repayment schedules

The structuring of the deal should never be "left to the financial people". All members of the team as well as all the financial backers should make sure that they understand the structure and its implications across a range of scenarios. It is also vital that there is full exchange of information between all parties so as to ensure that all sides are working to the same assumptions.

Clear Exit Route

Many structures prove to be sound but the deal fails to live up to expectations because the team and its backers have not clearly thought out their exit route. The structure of most MBO's depends upon an ultimate sale of the business and the capital gain thereby generated is usually a significant component of the overall return. Most institutions will formulate an exit strategy before backing a buy-out and it is worthwhile for a management team to ensure that their ideas on exits correlate to those of the institutions.

And so having looked at the perfect buy-out let us now move on to look at the process in more detail.

The steps involved

Establishing the principle

The idea of executing a management buy-out may emanate from the management team itself, from the parent company or from a third party, such as a venture capitalist or a corporate financier. The first objective for the management team, regardless of whoever made the initial suggestion, should be to gain agreement from the vendor that the business is for sale. This will be relatively straightforward if the vendor has suggested the disposal to the management, or, if the parent company has announced that it is considering selling the business – indeed, it has not been uncommon for management teams to learn that their business is for sale through such company announcements.

Whatever the circumstances, the management team should declare its interest at an early stage. Subsidiary directors who are contemplating a management buy-out may feel reluctant to disclose their intentions early on, but this will almost certainly put them at risk of breaching their contracts of employment – and their fiduciary obligations as directors – as they face a number of significant conflicts of interest. These are reviewed in more depth in Chapter Eight, but managements should be aware that they:

– are under a duty not to disclose confidential information to third parties, as this could damage the business of the company and affect the price that the vendors may be able to obtain for their shares;
– may be called upon to vote at board meetings on major issues affecting the company, which may also be issues that affect the likelihood of a management buy-out;
– should not involve any of their colleagues in a management buy-out or persuade staff to join the buy-out vehicle.

These conflicts of interest should be capable of resolution, providing there is adequate disclosure by the management team. The team should certainly obtain the approval of the parent company before making any approach to an independent financial adviser or a venture capitalist.

Businesses are sold for a variety of reasons, many of which influence the negotiating position of the vendor. This situation represents a further conflict of interest for the management team, who will wish to pursue self-interest and negotiate the lowest possible purchase price. However, they are negotiating with their employer, whose interests they are expected to represent and with whom relationships may have to be maintained – either because the sale may fall through, or because of trading relationships that will continue after the buy-out. The relationship with the seller therefore demands skilful handling throughout the transaction.

The initial approach to the vendor may be informal, such as a visit by the leader of the management team to the chief executive of the parent company outside office hours; or it may be formal, and take the shape of a written proposal to the board of the directors. In either case, the management team has four aims:

– to declare its interest in acquiring the business;
– to ensure that they will be taken seriously as prospective purchasers;
– to begin tentative price negotiations;
– to obtain permission to approach a third party adviser on a confidential basis.

The management will wish to emphasise to the vendor the attractions of selling to the management team, rather than pursuing a competitive auction. The principal attractions may be summarised as follows:

Competitive price The management should be able to afford a competitive price unless the target company has a special value to a trade buyer; for example, if the trade buyer is in the same sector then it may be able to achieve significant cost savings by combining the business with its own.

Confidentiality. The management team can offer the vendor complete confidentiality, as only professional financiers and advisers will be involved. The potential dangers of a trade sale, which may lead to the closest competitors of the business being provided with detailed information on the business and even being escorted round the company's production facilities, should be pointed out to the parent company.

Speed. The management's knowledge of the business puts them in a position to act very quickly, and the management buy-out market enables funds to be raised in a short space of time.

Familiarity. The vendor may wish to have a continuing trading relationship with the business which is to be sold, and may feel more confident dealing with incumbent management.

Reduced warranties. It is likely that the vendor will be able to avoid giving extensive warranties and indemnities to a management buy-out vehicle, although certain warranties will need to be given.

Participation. The vendor may be offered the opportunity to participate in the equity or the debt of the management buy-out vehicle. This may help allay any fears the vendor may have that the subsequent performance of the business, or a high profile flotation that results in a substantial capital gain for the management, will embarrass the vendor by suggesting that the business was sold too cheaply.

Only option. The very fact that the management have made a formal bid for the business may reduce its value in the eyes of other would-be purchasers; it suggests to an alternative buyer that, if successful, they might face an unmotivated management team and a hostile workforce. It may also be that there are no alternative purchasers, or that the business is so dependent on its senior management that the need to satisfy their ambitions is overriding.

Costs The sale of the business through an auction is likely to give rise to a much higher level of fees for the vendor than an agreed management buy-out.

If the vendor is convinced that the management are potential purchasers, the team should seek to obtain a first option over the business and a period of exclusivity (although the vendor is likely to resist these suggestions).

Appointing a financial adviser

Once the possibility of a buy-out has been established, it is customary for the team to recruit an independent financial adviser. Members of a management buy-out team are unlikely to perform more than one buy-out during their working lives, and appropriate advice at an early stage is sensible when embarking on such a complex and sophisticated transaction. In addition, the members of the team will find themselves under immense pressure and severe time constraints during the buy-out process, as well as having to fulfil their continuing management responsibilities; the financial adviser is invaluable in mitigating this burden.

The corporate finance departments of the larger accounting firms now play a major role in the provision of independent advice to management buy-out teams, although lawyers and independent corporate financiers may often be found acting in this role. The adviser must have proven expertise and experience of such transactions, and should be someone with whom the management team is comfortable (since they will be required to work closely with him or her over a long period of time).

The financial adviser will play a number of different roles during the course of the buy-out, and these may be summarised as follows:

- preparation of a feasibility study of the buy-out opportunity;
- advice on the preparation of a detailed business plan;
- preparing an outline financial structure for the buy-out;
- identifying and negotiating with equity investors;
- identifying and negotiating with bank financiers;
- negotiating with the vendor;
- providing advice on the price to be paid for the business;
- dealing with the complex tax and accounting issues arising from a buy-out;
- providing financial management advice on treasury issues, such as interest rate and foreign currency exposure management;
- assisting in the orchestration of the buy-out process to a successful completion.

A good commercial lawyer with buy-out experience will be required to complete the buy-out team. The lawyer should also be appointed at an early stage, and certainly before an offer letter is drafted to the vendor outlining the proposed acquisition terms.

The financial adviser will normally be prepared to work substantially on a contingent fee basis – particularly in the early stages. It is essential that clear agreement is reached as to who shall bear the costs if the transaction does not proceed. The management team should seek to use professional advisers effectively, as they will be incurring significant success fees. A detailed plan should be drawn up as to how the workload involved in the transaction will be shared. Although good teamwork will help to ease this workload, the management should never underestimate the extent of the demands on their time, and will need to plan how the business will be run during the period that their time and energies are absorbed with the transaction. A high level of pre-planning for meetings, and prior preparation of the information and documentation required by advisers, will help to ensure that their time is used effectively.

The feasibility study

The first task of the independent financial adviser is to conduct a feasibility study of the proposal in order to assess whether the management team should proceed. This feasibility study may be based on the first draft of the business plan that the management team have prepared, or on an existing corporate plan – although neither of these documents is absolutely necessary in order for an experienced financial adviser to make a quick assessment. The advisor will wish to cover the areas outlined below.

The business
The advisor will wish to examine:

- historic and current performance;
- financial projections;
- balance sheet strength;
- product profile and market position;
- reliance on major customers or suppliers;
- reliance on parent;
- ability to operate independently from the parent company; and
- the existence of any surplus assets which will not be required by the buy-out vehicle.

The management
The following questions will need to be answered:

- is the buy-out team a complete management team, with all the necessary skills to run an independent business?
- what is their track record?
- has the leader of the management team been identified?

- what level of personal financial resources is the team prepared to commit to the buy-out?
- does the team have the determination and enthusiasm to see the buy-out through?
- who will take part in the detailed buy-out process and who will ensure that the business continues to function properly while the deal is happening?

The price

The essential questions are:

- what is the price range likely to be required by the parent company?
- can that price be supported by a leveraged buy-out vehicle?
- how strong is the negotiating position of the management team?
- are favourable deferred consideration terms possible?

Working capital

The working capital requirements and capital expenditure plans of the target company are of crucial importance:

- can these requirements be met by the management buy-out vehicle?
- can the working capital requirements of the business be managed more effectively?
- can other forms of finance be used to meet capital expenditure requirements?
- can capital expenditure plans be deferred?

Potential competition

This area poses some of the most difficult questions:

- will there be competitive bidders for the business?
- what might be they be prepared to pay for the business?
- does the company have any special value to potential trade buyers?
- what particular advantages do the management team have in comparison?

The feasibility study should be carried out fairly quickly, and may even be completed within a day or two. If the conclusion of the financial adviser is that a management buy-out is practical, the next step will be for the management team to prepare a detailed business plan. The financial adviser will, meanwhile, prepare a timetable and begin planning approaches to potential financiers.

The business plan

The main objective of the business plan is to help raise finance, but it may also serve as an aid memoire to management in focusing their minds on their ambitions for the business and how to achieve them. A clear, concise, well-presented business plan is an important factor in securing investor confidence in the management team and the buy-out proposal. To do this, the plan should:

- attract the financier's interest and attention;

– emphasise the strengths of the business and its position in the market, especially as compared to its competitors;

– recognise the risks; and

– project the development of the business.

The financial forecasts are a critical part of the plan. Consideration should be given as to how each piece of information in the plan affects the plausibility of the forecasts, as these forecasts provide the information on which institutions make their initial investment decision. The plan should also help to establish both the price for the business and the structure for the transaction.

The business plan should not presume that the reader has any prior knowledge of the business, but must explain the proposal from basic premises; it should avoid jargon and excessive technical detail. The plan should be brief: most are no longer than 15 – 20 pages. A balance needs to be struck between ensuring that the document is concise and well-presented, and providing sufficient information. The financier will often conduct his own investigation, and therefore will not always need detailed explanations at this stage – any detailed information regarded as essential should be provided as appendices. Where possible, reference should be made to external data or publications to support the information given; unsupported opinions and assertions show a lack of preparation and professionalism.

There are no hard-and-fast rules as to the contents of the business plan, but the financial adviser – who is able to distance himself from the business – will provide objective advice on the contents and drafting of the plan. However, the management team should not expect the financial adviser to write the business plan. Potential investors will wish to read the thoughts and philosophy of the individuals in whom they may invest – they are not proposing to invest in the financial adviser. Detailed assistance may be provided if the preparation of the financial projections involves computer models, as financial advisers usually have considerable resources in this area. The management team should try to understand the needs of the venture capitalist, and particularly his or her requirements in terms of information. Particular attention should be paid to presentation; approximately 95% of business plans are rejected, and this is often because their presentation lets them down. A business plan will be expected to address the areas outlined in the panel below.

ELEMENTS OF A BUSINESS PLAN

- executive summary

- business

- management

- markets and marketing

- competition

- customers

- products and product development

- production

- suppliers

- location

- strategy for future development

- financial analysis

- management reporting systems

- exit routes

The executive summary listed at the top of the panel is a key factor in attracting the interest of a financier – who may be required to review many such plans each week. The summary should include a brief description of the business, its recent results and financial projections, an estimate of the finance needed for the management buy-out, and the objectives of the buy-out team.

Agreeing a price

Many text books have been written on the subject of the valuation of unquoted companies. However, in simple terms, agreeing a price for the target business is a matter of arriving at a figure which is acceptable to the vendor and which also represents good value for the purchaser – usually through face-to-face negotiation. The compromise reached through negotiation must then be compared with the range of values that the buy-out vehicle is able to afford. There can be an overwhelming temptation for management to offer a price which will secure a deal, but which is beyond the ability of the forecast profits and cash flows of the buy-out vehicle to finance. This is, perhaps, the most common feature of failed management buy-outs. In practice, the financial adviser and, indeed, the financiers and bankers, should ensure that any inclination to overbid is resisted and that the maximum price which can be supported by the management buy-out vehicle is not exceeded. The detailed process involved in structuring a deal is dealt with in Chapter Three. However, it is worth examining here some of the issues and factors which will affect a price level that is considered by the vendor to be acceptable, or by a purchaser to be good value, before looking in detail at how one might calculate the price that a buy-out vehicle could afford.

The vendor's position

The vendor may be influenced by some or all of the factors detailed below when deciding what is an acceptable price:

– In the case of a public company, the impact of the disposal on earnings is important. The vendor may be less price sensitive when considering the disposal of a loss making subsidiary; even if the loss-maker is disposed of for a token sum, representing a significant discount to asset value, this would represent an enhancement of the public company's earnings.
– The vendor's need for cash can often be an overriding requirement, and the timing of the cash inflow arising from the disposal may be important; in this situation, the speed with which a deal can be completed may be crucial.
– The value of the target company to any other potential competing bidders will have a significant influence on the vendor's price expectations.
– If the only alternative facing the vendor is closure of the business, involving heavy asset write-downs, redundancy costs and trading losses as the business is run down, it may prove possible for management to acquire the business at a considerable discount to book value.
– If the business is heavily dependent on individual members of the management team, and it is a realistic option for them to start up a new business in competition with the target, the vendor will be more inclined to agree a price at the lower end of the range of possible values, and less inclined to entertain third-party bidders.

The management team's position

The value of the target business is largely determined by its ability to provide appropriate investment returns to the team and its backers, in the light of both the perceived commercial risks of the business, and of the financial risks arising in the buy-out vehicle. This ability is clearly dependent on the capacity of the business to generate future profits and cash flows – asset values are generally of secondary importance.

The financial adviser will be able to form a view as to a realistic value for the business, having regard to historical and projected financial information. This value may be influenced by particular attributes of the target, such as:

– exceptional products or product developments;
– a strong or weak market position;
– an excellent management team;
– undue reliance on a limited number of customers or suppliers; and
– a market which is growing, static or declining.

These factors will not only influence the value which may be attributed to the business, but will also enable the venture capitalist to form a view of the level of risk which is being assumed.

Structuring a buy-out

Chapter Three deals with the practical considerations of structuring a buy-out and looks at some examples. The external funding for a typical management buy-out is likely to come from a combination of some, or all, of four principal sources:

– secured debt providers;
– mezzanine debt providers;
– equity investors;
– vendor finance.

Secured debt

Secured debt is the cheapest form of institutional finance available to the management team. Senior debt will generally represent the main source of acquisition funding, taking the form of a term loan with fixed repayment terms.

Secured debt providers may also advance working capital facilities to the company. These will usually be intended to fund cyclical cash flows arising from seasonal trading patterns – for example, in the case of an importer of gifts which are largely sold at Christmas.

Mezzanine finance

Mezzanine finance is an increasingly common feature of larger buy-outs. It is simply debt that is subordinated to – that is, ranks behind – senior debt in its rights to security. Mezzanine debt is often repaid when the company is sold or floated, rather than according to a medium-term repayment schedule. Mezzanine finance is riskier than senior debt, as less security and less cash flow is devoted to it; it therefore commands a higher rate of return, often in the region of 18 per cent to 20 per cent per annum.

Institutional equity providers

The providers of institutional equity, or venture capitalists, require returns that are substantially in excess of the cost of senior debt or mezzanine finance; these higher returns reflect the greater level of risk borne by an equity investment. In the case of a typical management buy-out of a sound business, the institution may expect an annual compound return of upwards of 30 per cent per annum. This required rate of return will reflect the perceived risk level of the business, and can be used to judge the relative attractions of competing investment proposals. The institutional investors will measure potential and actual success by reference to the internal rate of return (IRR), which is the rate of return on their total investment represented by the discounted value of future income and capital cash flows.

Vendor finance

Vendor finance may take the form of a subordinated loan, preference shares or, occasionally, an equity interest. Such "deferred" consideration, especially when it carries a right to equity involvement, can help bridge any price gap that remains after the negotiations; it also allows the vendor to secure a higher "headline" price for presentation to third parties when it announces the disposal. The deferred consideration may be payable only when a particular event occurs in the future that underpins the higher price.

Vendors may also provide non-loan means of assistance to the divested subsidiary – for instance, a rent-free period for their existing premises, or the guarantee of a certain level of turnover if there is mutual trading. A level of ongoing involvement by the vendor can help to maintain confidence among suppliers and customers of the newly independent buy-out vehicle.

Other sources of finance may include leasing, hire purchase, factoring and invoice discounting. Management may also be able to effect improvements in working capital management, a reduction in stock levels or debtor days, and the extension of levels of credit from suppliers; all of these measures have the potential to generate cash resources for the buy-out vehicle.

A practical example of the structuring of a typical management buy-out is appended to this chapter.

Approaching and choosing backers

There are no hard-and-fast rules as to whether a management team should approach financial backers prior to detailed negotiations with the vendor, or after such detailed negotiations have been completed. Certainly, the management team and their professional adviser should have a broad indication of the price range that will be acceptable to the vendor prior to approaching any financial backers. It is very difficult for financiers to assess an investment proposal without an indicative price.

The position of the management team may be significantly enhanced if it has already secured conditional financial backing before sitting down to agree a price with the vendor. Provisional financial backing can be particularly useful if the management team is expecting to face competition from other buyers, or if the vendor seems inclined to oppose any buy-out proposal. Securing provisional financial backing can remove one of the vendor's principal concerns: that the buy-out team will be unable to raise the money, but, whilst they pursue the opportunity, other potential buyers may be lost and the value of the business may diminish.

General principles

The management team should be guided by their professional adviser, who will have a wide range of contacts amongst financiers. The professional adviser will be able to introduce the team to those backers whose investment criteria are most likely to match the financial requirements of the management team. The expertise of the financial adviser is needed to ensure that a number of potentially conflicting objectives are met. Notably, the management team will wish to secure financial backing quickly, as the buy-out opportunity may be short-lived, but at the same time they will wish to entertain a number of competing offers to ensure that they obtain the best deal possible.

The market for the provision of finance to management buy-outs is fiercely competitive, and it is likely that a team with a strong proposal will be faced with a choice of competing offers. Many teams then make a decision that is based on the personal chemistry which has arisen between themselves and the potential backers. The importance of this criteria should not be underestimated, not least because it is impossible to "sack" an equity partner in the event of disagreement – as is possible with other advisers. More importantly, the team will be working very closely and intensely with their backers, and mutual understanding and common aims amongst the various parties are the key to a successful management buy-out.

Equity investors

The first task will be to appoint a principal institutional investor (or "lead investor"). A lead investor may be expected to provide all of the equity funds for a smaller buy-out, but will look to involve other equity investors on larger deals. This involvement is usually arranged before, but sometimes after, completion; the process is called syndication. Generally, individual equity institutions wish to own less than 50 per cent of the new company and are more comfortable with about 30 per cent, as this will enable them to advance further funds in the future for expansion or to finance acquisitions without the buy-out vehicle becoming a direct subsidiary.

The lead equity investor or venture capitalist will play an active role in the buy-out process. This role may include some or all of the following:

– evaluating the target to ensure that adequate investment returns will be provided, and that a deal is likely to be completed at an acceptable price;
– working on the financial structure of the buy-out with the financial advisers;
– providing equity capital and arranging equity capital from other venture capitalists in the event of a syndication;
– helping to arrange other types of funding;
– leading negotiations between the institutional investors and the management team;
– assisting in negotiations with the vendor;
– undertaking due diligence and instructing the reporting accountants;
– monitoring subsequent performance on behalf of institutional investors;
– providing post-investment support;
– handling the exit.

The choice of a lead investor involves matching the financial requirements of the management team with those of the lead investor to ensure that each party has compatible objectives. An experienced professional adviser will be aware of the various investment criteria and the differing requirements of potential lead investors, and will introduce the management team to those institutions whose criteria are most suitable. The following factors commonly influence the choice:

Exit strategies. In general, venture capitalists are looking for a medium-term capital gain within a period of three to five years, and will expect to achieve an exit through flotation or trade sale. There will be no difficulty if the management team has a shorter investment horizon. However, some management teams may have longer-term horizons, stretching to seven or more years, and a more limited range of investors will be appropriate for these teams.

Overall return. Some institutions place more emphasis on running yields (that is, the payment of dividends during the life of an investment), than others. If the cash generation profile of the buy-out vehicle will not allow for the payment of high running yields, the management team is obviously more likely to reach an acceptable deal with an equity investor who is more interested in capital gain. Alternatively, the business profile may lend itself more readily to the payment of a high running yield, and the management team might prefer to work with an investor who is less interested in a relatively quick exit by trade sale or flotation.

Investor involvement. Institutions differ in the degree to which they wish to be involved with the buy-out vehicle after an investment has been made. Some prefer a "hands off" approach, in which the involvement of the equity investor after the buy-out is restricted to having one or two nominated non-executive directors on the board. Other institutions offer a much higher level of support ("hands on"), and this can be attractive to management teams who suddenly find themselves in an independent, and thus unfamiliar, corporate environment. A non-executive director with experience of the buy-out vehicle's sector, and who can add value through business contacts, may be appointed to the board; a venture capitalist may offer proactive corporate advice on a more regular basis.

Secondary funding. An ambitious management buy-out team may wish to raise further funding, in the medium term, for the expansion of the business or to make an acquisition. In this case an equity backer who commands sufficient investment funds to be able to invest in further rounds of finance will be an advantage, as it is a much more straightforward process to arrange finance from existing investors than it is to approach third parties.

Transaction size. All providers of institutional equity finance have investment size criteria. Only a limited number of institutions are prepared to finance management buy-outs below a value of £1 million. On the other hand, at the larger end of the scale (over £50 million), there are, again, only a limited number of venture capitalists with the appropriate experience and funding resources.

Experience is also a key factor when choosing a financial backer. The backer should have experience of complex management buy-outs, and also a technical and commercial understanding of the particular business sector in which the business will operate. The management team should take up references on the venture capitalist, and speak to other management teams with whom the financier has worked. They should certainly ensure that the venture capitalist has a successful track record.

Assessing the backer

Initial meetings between the management team and potential backers are two-way processes. The management team is seeking to make a strong first impression and enthuse the backer with their proposal. However, in turn the potential backer is trying to impress the management team; in an increasingly competitive market, a wide variety of sources of finance is now available to the management team.

It has already been mentioned that one important criterion is personal chemistry. The management team should also check that the backer has carefully read their business plan, and is taking their proposal seriously. Does the backer demonstrate an understanding of, and an enthusiasm for, their business? The process of choosing a backer may extend over a number of meetings, and the team will want to satisfy themselves on a number of points:

- Will the backer be able to devote the time necessary speedily to complete a complex transaction.
- Is the backer easily accessible?
- Does the backer have the necessary resources to meet the needs of the management team?
- Is their contact a key decision maker? Or does he or she have to cope with layers of authority within the institution?

These criteria apply equally well to bankers and mezzanine financiers, as well as equity providers. In addition, it may be necessary to consider whether the banker has expert knowledge of a specialist sector, for example commodity trading, and can provide specialist financial instruments, or the banking arrangements and facilities that the business may require. The management team should bear all these factors in mind, and not be guided solely by the financial terms of each offer. It may well be that the most competitive offer with regard to the management's share of the buy-out vehicle, or the keenest interest rates on senior debt, will not represent the best choice.

Negotiating with the vendor

The aim of negotiations with the vendor is to fix the purchase price for the target business and, subsequently, to agree the detailed terms, conditions, warranties and indemnities relating to the acquisition.

Who should lead the negotiations on the management side? This may be a member of the management team, a professional financial adviser or the lead investor, and it is worth considering the relative merits of each party:

The leader of the management team. The team leader may historically have a strong relationship with those conducting negotiations on behalf of the vendor. On the other hand, he may feel uncomfortable negotiating with his employer, particularly given that the sale may fall through. The team leader may not possess the necessary negotiating skills and experience, and may welcome the opportunity to be distanced from a face-to-face confrontation.

Lead investor. The lead investor may be expected to possess all the advantages of an independent negotiator – and has the additional advantage of financial credibility in the eyes of the vendor. The lead investor will also be in a position to exert firm control over the price negotiations.

Financial adviser. The adviser can provide an impersonal interface between the management team and the vendor, and should certainly possess the appropriate negotiating skills. As an outsider, the financial adviser may be in a better position to drive a hard bargain. Furthermore, the financial adviser is in a position, when an impasse has been reached, to refer to the management team for further instructions; this enables the team to compromise on an issue without losing face.

Whoever leads the negotiating team, the normal ground rules of effective negotiation apply. The team should ensure that intransigent positions are not adopted, and that empty threats are not made – for example, that the management team will resign if the negotiations are not successful! The leader should maintain the negotiations at an appropriate pace, and ensure that meetings are properly minuted; notes should be circulated to all parties to confirm what has been agreed.

Strategy

Planning is critical to a successful negotiation. The negotiating team should spend a considerable amount of time beforehand assessing the strengths and weaknesses of both their position and that of the vendor. Some of the factors which may influence those positions have already been outlined. The team should also have a clear idea of what is being acquired. The target may comprise a company or group of companies, or a collection of assets and a business which represents a division of a company rather than a separate legal entity. The buy-out vehicle may occasionally be given the opportunity to acquire either shares or assets; the team should take appropriate professional advice if this is the case. Generally, medium-sized and large management buy-outs are share purchases.

The team should identify the key issues that need to be resolved, in addition to the price. These include:

– liabilities to be assumed by the buy-out vehicle;
– capital expenditure commitments;
– pension scheme funding and future arrangements;
– contingent liabilities;
– reliance on group services;
– intragroup funding, and the resolution of any outstanding balances on completion.

Negotiations can become tense and heated, and there is a danger of jealousy on the part of fellow executives involved in negotiations on the other side. The team must maintain a calm and professional approach, and encourage all parties to work together to overcome any hurdles which arise in a logical and effective manner. Provided that the indicative price offered by the management is approximately correct, the early stages of negotiation will be taken up with haggling to bridge any gap between the price offered by the management and that expected by the vendor. Subsequently, price may tend to be overshadowed by subsidiary factors. Management should make the most of a potential advantage that they have: they can understand and quantify certain problems with the business, which may make the business less attractive to a competing bidder.

Heads of agreement

Although instructions may be given to lawyers to produce a draft sale and purchase agreement as soon as possible, this may take some time, and it is common practice to document the outcome of the negotiations in summary form. This summary of what has been agreed is often called "heads of agreement" or "memorandum of understanding". Although heads of agreement are not normally legally binding, care should be exercised and legal advice sought, as they represent a clear expression of the intent to proceed made by each party. Furthermore, it can prove difficult to re-negotiate something which has been documented in the heads of agreement, even if it was not what the management team had originally intended.

The team should seek to obtain a period of exclusivity from the vendor, during which time the vendor will not entertain offers from competing bidders. This will allow the buy-out to proceed through the due diligence and legal documentation stages without undue risk and pressure. Strict confidentiality is likely to be a requirement of both parties during this period, and no public announcements should be made without the prior agreement of all concerned.

Vendors will often agree, upon commencement of due diligence, to underwrite some element of the professional fees which will now be incurred by the management team. This underwriting of fees may be restricted to certain circumstances – for example, if the vendor decides to withdraw from the transaction.

From this point in the management buy-out, much time will be spent with the lawyers who are drafting the necessary documentation; the detailed legal considerations which will arise are considered in Chapter Eight.

Structuring the transaction

Introduction

In this chapter we discuss the theoretical basis used by providers of capital to structure a transaction. This is done by means of a theoretical deal based on a company, TargetCo, and by some real examples of deals from recent years.

Components of the MBO funding structure

The equity provider or institution will usually establish an outline structure with the assistance of the team's financial advisers. In most buy-outs, the funds will come from a mixture of some or all of:

– senior debt
– mezzanine
– institutional equity
– vendor financing
– management equity

   The principle applied by any provider of finance is that the potential reward to the provider of capital must match the risk the provider takes. In buy-outs the complication is that there are often several layers of funding all with various rights and rankings. And of course, whilst the theory for structuring a deal is straightforward, the practice is complicated by the fact that no two deals are ever the same.

Assessing the financial profile of the business

Whatever the industry, the institutions will in every case need to start by assessing the cash flow and asset characteristics of the company it is looking to fund. The funding structure must then be tailored to meet this profile. You would not acquire a house with a 3 year loan or a car on a 25 year mortgage. The same rules apply when financing the buy-out, or buy-in, of a company.

This matching of the cash generative life of an asset with the term of the financing used to purchase it is an old established financing principle and is the base rationale behind any financial structure. To assess the assets and cash generative profile of a company, the institutions will typically request that the management team prepare detailed forecasts over a three to five year period for the business. These are key to determining the price the institution should be willing to pay for the business. It is therefore imperative that they are as well founded as possible so as to enable the institutions to take an initial view of whether they are reasonable. If the future looks very different from the past, alarm bells will start ringing. Projections with hockey stick profiles are rarely achieved.

Once the institution is happy with the projected future cash flows and profits of the business, a financing model can be structured around the financial profile going forward.

Example of a Theoretical Structure – TargetCo

Every deal will have its own particular features but there are certain rules of thumb which can be followed in most cases. The best way to illustrate how these rules are applied is to take a theoretical example and work down through the different types and rankings of capital.

TargetCo is a manufacturer of canned fruit. The product is sold in supermarkets throughout the UK. As such its earnings are not volatile and there is an expectation that it will benefit from the continuing consolidation in the supermarket chains. The business is well positioned in its marketplace.

TargetCo is currently owned by a UK plc, called VendorCo. Due to the recession, VendorCo is under pressure to raise money. Its share price has slumped and hence equity markets are not attractive. It is therefore looking to raise money by selling non-core subsidiaries.

TargetCo is run autonomously from VendorCo and has a strong in situ management team that want to do a buy-out. However, it is anticipating high capital expenditure in future years as a result of increasingly strict EC standards and the exacting requirements of the supermarkets. Consequently, TargetCo has a financial profile as shown in Exhibit 1.

Exhibit 1 TargetCo Financial Profile

Year Ended 30 September	Actual 1994 £m	Projections 1995 £m	1996 £m
Sales	23.6	25.9	28.0
Trading Profits	1.9	2.2	2.6
Sales Growth	12.8 %	9.8 %	8.1 %
Trading Margin	8.1 %	8.5 %	9.3 %
Capital Expenditure	0.8	1.0	1.2
Free Cash Flow	1.6	1.9	2.0

It is clear that the business is profitable and that management believe that there are real growth prospects. The capital spending programme is quite demanding in terms of the cash it will require, although this is allowing the trading margins to improve over the life of the projections. The funding institutions have done their due diligence and are satisfied that these projections are a reasonable Base Case with which to work.

The institutions like the business and believe that it will be a saleable or floatable entity in three to four years. From looking at comparable companies and TargetCo's growth prospects, a price equivalent to a price earnings multiple of around 12 seems reasonable. The institutions are therefore willing to bid say £15m. The costs of doing a deal of this size (i.e. legal fees, accounting fees, underwriting fees, arrangement fees, etc.) tend to be in the region of £300,000 to £500,000 and our total finance requirement is therefore £15.5 million.

How much senior debt can be raised?

The first step is to decide how much senior debt can be raised to support the price. The process by which the provider of senior debt decides how much financing he is prepared to provide is dealt with in Chapter Four. Whilst, as pointed out in that chapter, there is no little black book of rules determining the answer here, when structuring a deal it will be necessary to make certain assumptions. For example, the equity provider will usually assume that a senior lender will typically be lending at a margin of around 2 per cent plus an arrangement fee.

On margins this tight, the lender will take a more pessimistic view of the projections to that of an equity provider. He is therefore likely to take a reasonable set of Base Case projections, adjust them downwards for the possibility of events working against the company, and then still want to be satisfied that the loan can be serviced and repaid. It is this adjusted case, the Downside Case, that will determine the level of funding that a bank will be prepared to extend to a transaction.

TargetCo is a typical MBO structure and the senior lenders will therefore be looking to satisfy the standard lending criteria for MBOs. Standard gearing in today's market for MBOs is around 50 per cent and TargetCo's earnings, being food based, are not deemed to be volatile.

Exhibit 2 How much senior debt?

Uses:	£000	Sources:	£000
Purchase Price	15,000	Senior Debt	7,500
Fees and Expenses	500	Resulting equity requirement	8,000
Total	15,500		15,500

The debt provider will usually need to be satisfied that the debt can be repaid in seven years although this is likely to be back-ended to allow for the capital expenditure programme. In addition, he will want to be satisfied that there is prudent asset coverage. TargetCo is a manufacturing business that is rich in assets; it has a strong debtor covenant in that its principal debtors are the UK supermarket chains. It may therefore be fair to assume that a senior lender will be satisfied that his asset risk is low.

The senior lender will also wish to be satisfied that his covenant risk (i.e. the likelihood of a company being unable to service its debts) is low. A widely used measure of this is interest cover and a rule of thumb is that a banker would wish to see interest covered by operating profits by at least two times in the first year with incremental increases thereafter. He will also look to see that the operating cash flow cover is comfortable.

Assuming a level of senior debt of £7.5 million, and looking at the effect on projected profits and cash flows, TargetCo appears able to satisfy these parameters. The senior lender should therefore be happy to provide £7.5m, or roughly half the funding. This leaves £8m to be obtained from elsewhere.

Mezzanine Finance

Moving down the funding layers, we come to the non-debt elements of the finance.

As the senior lender does not intend to take more than a marginal risk, the allocation of risk, and reward, has to be spread between the remaining parties. Usually these will be the management team, the provider of institutional equity, the vendor (if they are maintaining an ongoing interest) and possibly mezzanine.

Mezzanine is finance consisting of any mixed form financial instrument layered in a company's capital structure between equity and senior debt. In other words unquoted capital which ranks in terms of risk, return and security between senior debt and share capital. Mezzanine finance seeks to exploit the opportunity created by the substantial difference which exists between the risk/reward profile of senior debt and equity finance. It is usually provided in the form of a subordinated loan with equity warrants which crystallise at the sale of the company. Generally it is priced to yield an IRR over three to five years in the high teens to low twenties – roughly half way between the standard expectations of the senior debt and institutional equity providers. The mezzanine loan usually has a high yield of 3 to 4.5 per cent over LIBOR.

Thus mezzanine is a hybrid of debt and equity with a hybrid return. However, most providers of mezzanine regard it as an instrument with characteristics that are closer to that of debt than equity. It will generally have entitlement to a fixed current yield and therefore in a default situation is entitled to interest and principal. The holder also often has the right to put a company into liquidation.

DETERMINANTS OF MEZZANINE CAPACITY

- Low volatility in earnings but projections do assume market growth
- Due to the need to invest in capex, senior debt repayments are back ended
- Capex investment is assumed to bring about increases in trading margins
- Don't wish identified Commercial Risks to be compounded by Financial Risks

Mezzanine is used as a bridge between the price expectation of sellers and the returns required by the institutional equity providers. It is reasonably flexible in terms of term and interest payments – a mezzanine instrument can often be structured to have a deferred yield to allow, say, high capital expenditure. This is not something that a senior debt provider would be willing to do. It can be a cost effective use of funds as it lowers the amount of more expensive equity that is required in a transaction, and therefore the percentage of the company the institutional equity provider requires to achieve his desired return.

TargetCo's Mezzanine Capacity

If a strip of mezzanine is introduced into a structure, the provider should firstly satisfy himself that there is not volatility in the future earnings stream. Secondly, it is key that the risk taken is different from that of the equity provider so that the taking of a lower return is justified.

In the case of TargetCo, it is not necessary to have a strip of mezzanine funding. Due to the high asset coverage, senior lenders are providing half the funding. The gearing is therefore already reasonable at 50 per cent. Although the volatility in the earnings is low, management are forecasting growth on the back of supermarkets increasing their market share. Additionally margins are forecast to increase over time due to improvements in efficiency. There is a commercial risk that this growth and the efficiency improvements will not be realised.

Furthermore, TargetCo will be required by the EC and its customers, the supermarkets, to make year-on-year significant capital expenditure. This means that the senior debt repayment schedule will have to be back ended. If the institutions are to get a current yield on the institutional equity, and the institutions wish not to unduly compound the identified commercial risk with an increased financial risk, then we would not introduce mezzanine.

Exhibit 3 TargetCo's Mezzanine Capacity

Uses:	£000	Sources:	£000
Purchase Price	15,000	Senior Debt	7,500
Fees and Expenses	500	Mezzanine	0
		?	8,000
Total	15,500		15,500

This leaves the £8m gap to be filled by the various forms of equity.

The Equity Split

Equity funding will typically be provided in a buy-out from three sources: the institutions, management and, sometimes, the vendor. Regardless of the enthusiasm of a management team and its advisers and regardless of how much time, effort and money they are prepared to invest, the critical factor when looking to allocate equity between these participants, will be to satisfy the requirements of the institutional investor – if the equity provider is not happy, a deal is unlikely.

The Equity Provider – what return?

In general, the venture capital market is looking for compound returns in excess of 30 per cent per annum. In particular cases, when the risks are perceived to be higher than a standard buy-out, the return expectations are higher still. Why 30 per cent?

A fund manager running a portfolio of publicly quoted stock would regard that portfolio as being a success if over a decent interval of time it generated compound returns in the high teens to low twenties. As a provider of unquoted risk capital to a buy-out, the institutional investor is looking at a proposition which is inherently more risky than investing in quoted companies. He will therefore be looking for a premium to the fund manager, effectively to compensate for the higher failure rate. He will also be looking for compensation for the lack of liquidity in his share holdings.

Are these return expectations realistic? The interesting thing about them is that despite the fact that we have moved in recent years from a high interest rate, high inflation economy, to a low interest rate and low inflation environment, the returns which the institutional investors are seeking have not moved very much. This implies that the differential in return between investing in gilts and buy-outs has increased. The economy ought to be more stable and therefore the commercial risks in a buy-out should have decreased. However, research appears to suggest that the private equity industry has not significantly reduced its return expectations. At least not publicly!

The Institution's Share – Current yield vs. capital gain

Given the returns an institutional investor is looking for, how do we determine what proportion of the equity ought to go to the investor? As ever this goes back to the projections. By making an assumption about the likely exit date and multiple the venture capitalist can calculate what proportion of the company he will require to give him the desired return. In practice, this will usually be the result of trial and error involving extensive computer modelling. In assessing how much equity the company will support, the institution will balance the two elements making up the return – current yield and capital gain.

Current yield is the dividend stream that is received from the investment. This may take two forms, either a fixed dividend, usually attached to preference shares, or a participating dividend, usually attached to one class of share.

Capital gain is the appreciation in the value of the shareholding.

> **The Attractions of Current Yield**
>
> If a transaction is reasonably priced, the institutional investor should be able to receive a sensible current yield within 12-18 months of the investment being made. If not, it may be an indication that the price paid is too rich. But why should an institutional investor want to receive a current yield?
>
> Aside from covering the office costs, an investment that is structured with a current yield is inherently more attractive than one without. The reason for this is simple – compounding over the longer term is expensive. If an institution is looking to achieve a compound return of 30 per cent per annum without receiving a current yield then the capital value of its share holding has to more than double every three years. That is quite a task. Receiving a current yield helps forgive shortfalls in capital gain.
>
> However, different institutions have different levels of appetite for yield or capital gain. This is usually a function of how the institution itself is funded. A house which is funding its investments in the money market will need yield to satisfy the interest costs associated with your funding. On the other hand, a house with a large source of captive funds or which operates a fund with a plentiful supply of, say, pension fund investment, is likely to be less sensitive to the immediate future.

What type of equity?

The institutions will invest using any one or more of a number of instruments. Ordinary shares, preferred ordinary shares, cumulative preferred ordinary shares ('CPO's'), cumulative participating preferred ordinary shares ('CPPO's'), preference shares, redeemable preference shares, convertible shares and many other variations or combinations. However the three main categories are ordinary shares, preference shares and 'quasi equity' in the form of loan stock.

The bulk of the institutional equity will be in redeemable preference shares or loan stock, to enable the bulk of its investment to rank ahead of the ordinary shares in terms of redemption, dividends and shareholders rights. The institutional preferred equity, whether in preference shares or loan stock, is therefore a powerful instrument and strengthens the position of the institution.

The choice between preference shares and loan stock revolves around where they sit on the balance sheet. Loan stock will usually be classified as a liability, whereas preference shares will be part of the company's share capital and therefore will increase its balance sheet net worth. Most institutions are indifferent as to whether their share holding is in the form of preference shares or loan stock as they will take any current income gross. The pluses and minuses therefore relate much more to the effect on the company.

Because loan stock is classified as debt in the UK, the interest paid to the equity provider is usually tax deductible. Additionally, if there is a concern that there may not be sufficient distributable reserves to redeem preference shares, loan stock is attractive as it is not redeemed, but is repaid like any other debt. Reserves are therefore not an issue.

The downside to loan stock goes back to its classification as debt on the balance sheet. To the uninformed reader of the accounts the existence of loan stock on the balance sheet suggests high gearing and a limited equity cushion. The reader may well be a potential supplier to the company who could raise questions as to the creditworthiness of the company extending credit. This is a question of balance and needs to be looked at on a case by case basis.

Vendor Notes

Vendor notes have become increasingly prominent in management buy-outs and are now widely acknowledged as a standard ingredient in the funding cake. Vendor notes are also probably the most variable element in any structure. They can rank as first priority (ahead of all unsecured creditors) if they are in the form of a deferred consideration, or, as is more commonly the case, they can rank at the bottom of the heap, just ahead of management.

Increasingly, vendors are seeking to retain a share in the equity value of the company. They will therefore rank with the ordinary shareholders and the returns are tied together. The vendor is likely to regard this type of instrument as something of a punt on the business being able to increase its equity value. However, structurally, a loan note of this type will have a number of benefits to the vendor. It can allow him to dress up the headline price. It is harder to manipulate than a performance related note as he will share pound for pound with the ordinary shareholders at exit. Most of all it provides insurance. Even today many vendors may be distressed sellers, and as such may perceive that they are not selling out at the best time. An ongoing interest in the ordinary share capital gives them hope of retaining an interest in the upside. For publicly quoted companies this acts as a non-embarrassment clause. If the acquirer of a subsidiary brings that company back to the market in a short period of time at a super profit the vendor can at least claim to have participated in that profit and hence defend itself against the charge of having undersold the asset.

Management Equity

Last, but most definitely not least, we come to what is often the smallest, but always critical, component in the equity structure – the management's share. The various layers of capital that sit above the management stake are relying on the management team to deliver the projections and hence their returns. It therefore goes without saying that the management team will have to be properly incentivised to do so.

When the provider of institutional equity has determined his desired return and his preference for yield or capital gain, he can calculate what proportion of the equity he requires. The balance is then available for management. If that balance does not look large enough to provide the management team with an attractive deal, then it may well suggest that the price for the company is too high.

Of course, in the real world the process of deal structuring involves considerably more than deciding what is left for the management team. It may be that the team is shopping the deal around amongst many equity providers to see who will provide them with the best terms. In these circumstances the equity provider will be under pressure to provide the most competitive deal he can for management whilst ensuring that his institution is still keen to do the deal on those terms.

How much will management have to invest?

Once it is determined what proportion of the equity is available for management how does the venture capitalist assess how much they should pay for it? An industry rule of thumb is that if the management team is not already wealthy each member of the team should initially be prepared to contribute a sum equivalent to one and a half times his or her salary. This sum is sufficient to concentrate the mind, but is not so burdensome that it weighs the team down.

How to split the preference element

Determining the split between preference shares and ordinary shares is the last step in the equation. This is the arithmetical means by which the management proportion is determined. If management can commit a certain amount for their share of the ordinary equity, then the institutional share will be arrived at by investing an appropriate proportion of ordinary shares. For example, if management invest £200,000 for ordinary shares with 40 per cent of the voting rights, the institution will subscribe £300,000 for ordinary shares entitling it to 60 per cent of the voting rights. The balance, usually the bulk of the institutional capital, in the form of preference shares or loan stock.

There are of course endless variants on this process, the most obvious being the introduction of a ratchet. This is a mechanism whereby the amount of equity allocated to the management team is variable according to the performance of the company or the deal over time. For example, management's share of the equity might ratchet up if a certain pre-determined level of profit targets or market capitalisation can be achieved. This is a good way of incentivising management, particularly where there is a difference in perception of the achievability of the management projections between management and the institutional investor.

The underlying principle when designing the package for management is to ensure that they are motivated to provide the institutions with their return – i.e. what works for the institutions works for them.

Completing the TargetCo Structure

Let us now return to our working example of TargetCo. With £7.5m of funding from the senior debt providers, the bulk of the equity capital will be provided by the institutions. In order to achieve its target return of 30 per cent, based on a reasonable current yield of 7.5 per cent per annum, the institutional investors will require 90 per cent of the ordinary share capital. This implies that management will receive, initially, 10 per cent of the equity.

A three-member team with total annual earnings of £100,000, for example, gives a subscription price for management's 10 per cent of the equity, using our industry rule of thumb, of £150,000. If this obtains 10 per cent of the company, in the form of ordinary shares, then the other 90 per cent of the ordinary shares should cost £1,350,000.

These ordinary shares will be allotted to the equity institutions. The remaining equity requirement will be in the form of preference shares held by the institutions and thus the institutions will subscribe for preference shares of £6.0 million together with ordinary shares of £1.35 million

The completed structure is therefore as follows:-

Exhibit 4 Completed TargetCo Structure

Uses:	£000	Sources:	£000	% of Equity
Purchase price	15,000	Senior Debt	7,500	
Fees and Expenses	500	Mezzanine	0	
		Preference Shares	6,500	
		Institutional Ordinary	1,350	90
		Management Ordinary	150	10
	15,500		15,500	100

Some Real Examples

Let us now introduce the actual structuring of two real deals which involved Montagu Private Equity ('MPE'). Unlike TargetCo, these deals are not standard, but do give a feel for applying the company characteristics to the theory.

Case Study 1 – The Centric Pub Company

Centric Pub Company managed an estate of 200 tenanted pubs spread across the West Midlands and the North West of England. In March 1992, MPE led and structured the acquisition of this business by a buy-in team.

Exhibit 5 Centric Structure

Uses:	£000	Sources:	£000
Cost of Properties	22,500	Senior Bank Debt	14,300
Provision for remedial work	200	Subordinated Loan Stock	8,900
Costs and Fees	2,100	Ordinary Equity	1,600
	24,800		24,800

Principal Terms

- Senior Bank Debt has a 15 year term
- Loan Stock was effectively equity provided in a tax efficient manner
- Gearing level of 58 per cent

The business

Centric was formed in 1991 by John Hings and Paul Davies, in order to purchase a group of pubs from Bass plc. The pubs that Bass sold to Centric were not the flashy theme pubs which tend to have more volatile earnings as they go in and out of fashion. Instead they were the local boozers in their community. As such the clientele was loyal and their spending was highly predictable.

A further characteristic of the deal was that, for a buy-out, there was an unusually strong asset base. All the Bass pubs sold to Centric were either freehold or on long leases. The purchase price was determined by a notional price per pub and as such was overwhelmingly tied to property values rather than the businesss cash flow.

Level of gearing – a commercial risk profile

The characteristics of financing the acquisition of a pub are not so different from that of acquiring a home – MPE were just buying a lot of them. A house buyer does not expect his home to fall down, i.e. its useful life is long. However, he does expect to incur maintenance costs to make sure it remains standing and wants to be able to comfortably afford the monthly payments. He therefore arranges financing that matches its likely useful life and suits his available cash flow – probably mortgage financing with a 20-25 year term and low repayments of principal in the early years.

The financing of the Centric estate had exactly the same dynamics. Because the commercial risk was low – due to the relative lack of volatility in the earnings – it was possible to increase the level of gearing and hence, theoretically, the financial risk. The Midland Bank provided the company with 15-year money, on terms akin to a mortgage, although normally accustomed to lending on more standard 5-7 year terms. The level of gearing was relatively high at 58 per cent, but the Midland Bank assessed its covenant risk as low. Moreover, its asset risk was minimal due to its loan being underwritten by the property values of the pub portfolio. If the bank had stuck slavishly to the unwritten rule of a maximum term of 7 years for senior debt it would have broken the fundamental lending principal of matching the funding term to the useful life of the assets. This would have unnecessarily increased the financial risk to the detriment of the structure. The market for 15-year money is undoubtedly thin, but if the fundamentals of a deal demand longer term debt, it is available.

The Equity

The remaining bulk of the capital was in subordinated loan stock, with only 6 per cent being in the form of pure equity. As the captive arm of a world-wide banking group, Montagu Private Equity had no particular preference for loan stock or preference shares. The decision was therefore based on the projected level of cash and distributable reserves in the company itself.

Case Study 2 – Primary International Holdings Limited

This was a transaction which was at the other end of the spectrum in terms of structuring when compared with Centric. Centric's steady stream of cash flows contrasted dramatically with the sometimes erratic cash profile of primary. The contrasting risk profile was reflected in a very different deal structure.

Exhibit 6 Primary Structure

Uses:	£000	Sources:	£000
Purchase price	6,300	US Dollar Loan	7,000
Working Capital	3,000	Preference shares	2,700
Fees	700	Ordinary shares	100
		Cash balances	200
	10,000		10,000

Principal Terms

– US Dollar loan was provided by the institutional equity investors,
– No genuine debt in the acquisition structure, and
– No gearing.

The Business

Primary was owned by an American parent, the Golodetz Corporation, a privately owned US conglomerate with various metal trading and mining interests. In June 1992 Golodetz was looking to sell Primary, a profitable subsidiary and a steel and ferrous metal broker, with main offices in London, Dusseldorf and New York.

As with all trading businesses, the value of the business was very largely dependent on the market know-how of its key traders. If the traders wanted to buy the business it would have been relatively easy for them to frustrate another acquirer by threatening to leave. If a potential acquirer thought this threat real, the value of the company would have plummeted. This proved a useful weapon in agreeing a price with the vendor.

The commercial risk

Primary's core business was to act as a facilitator allowing steel producers to access difficult markets such as Algeria and Iran. It also acted as a conduit for minor countries to obtain a regular, uninterrupted supply of steel from the large steel mills who only find it economic to deal directly with very significant purchasers. For the period between taking and delivering the order

Primary was exposed to the risk of movements in steel prices. More importantly, perhaps, it also had exposure to the credit risk of the countries it has dealings with.

Despite the inevitable cycles in the steel market, under the stewardship of the traders, led by Pat Saiman, Primary had never made a loss since its foundation in the mid 1970s. Profits did fluctuate with the steel cycle, but had always remained in the $2-12.5m range. The steel cycle tends to be cyclical over an 8-10 year period. However, unlike other traded metals, steel prices fluctuate within a comparatively narrow envelope of plus and minus 10 per cent in any year.

No debt

The risk profile of Primary did not make it an easy transaction. The investors did not want to compound the commercial risk caused by a volatile earnings stream by gearing the funding structure and hence increasing the financial risk. As a result, the deal was financed with no genuine debt in the structure. A US dollar loan was advanced by the equity providers as a mechanism for redeeming capital as and when the company was able to, with the balance of the funding in the form of preferred and ordinary shares. The strip of dollar loan funding was called debt, but the reality was that in the minds of the providers all the funding was funding with an equity risk attached to it.

A good price

The fact that Golodetz was a forced seller and that the only plausible buyers were the management team meant that the team managed to buy the company at the knock down price earnings multiple of three times historic earnings. Even on very conservative projections MPE were allowed the luxury of not introducing a strip of real debt, whilst still anticipating a healthy equity return on the total funding, including the dollar loan.

A different structure

This case illustrates that if a standard MBO structure of roughly 50 per cent debt and 50 per cent equity had been employed it would not have been flexible enough to run with the potential volatility of the earnings stream. It is therefore vital that each transaction in analysed on a case by case basis.

Conclusions

As the theoretical structure and the real examples show, no two buy-out structures are the same. However, we can draw some conclusions.

Fit the deal to the company

The structure will always be tailored to the characteristics of the company. No structure can slavishly follow a standard model and management teams are advised to be wary of staking their bets on raising finance on a structure which fails to fully take into account the risk profile of a transaction.

Flexibility

The parties to the deal – be they equity or debt providers, advisers, the vendor or management – may have a very clear preference that they would want to see incorporated into any structure. An institution may perhaps prefer loan stock to preference shares or a vendor may insist on a certain form of vendor note. The structure will therefore change over the course of a deal and flexibility is important.

A fair deal

All participants in the funding structure must be getting a fair deal for the risks they are taking. A deal which fails to motivate the management team is a bad deal. At the same time, a deal that offers the equity provider insufficient returns to compensate it for taking the bulk of the equity risk, is unlikely to get beyond the Credit Committee.

A clear deal

Any deal must be understood by all the participants and be documentable. The participants, after having successfully concluded a deal, have subsequently found that, having reached for the Articles and the Investment Agreement at exit to determine the split of equity value, that a number of the parties to the deal apply different interpretations to the clauses. Clarity at an early stage saves a re-negotiation later.

There is always more than one solution. Institutions providing risk capital will take different views and will not come up with the same ideal structure. Each will have its own view of risk, which is always subjective, its own preference for yield or capital, and very often, a particular 'feel' for the risk, inherent in a particular industry.

The role of the banker

This chapter considers the role of the banker in management buy-outs and buy-ins. It is written from the point of view of a provider of bank debt and begins with an explanation of how a banker assesses the attractiveness and creditworthiness of a financing proposal; this is followed by a discussion of the principal debt and risk-hedging products that are likely to be required in a buy-out financing. The chapter concludes with a case study that illustrates the role of the banker in a typical transaction.

Assessing the proposal

The basic information necessary to encourage a bank to consider providing finance is the same whether the transaction be a buy-out or any other lending proposal. The aspects of a proposal that the bank will normally review – summarised by the classic banker's mnemonic CAMPARI – are discussed below.

Character

Who is the bank financing? Whether it is a loan to an individual or a large corporate concern, the same considerations apply. Integrity and track record are very high on the banker's agenda. The calibre of the borrower and the quality of marketing, technical and financial management will be closely scrutinised. If an entrepreneur has abandoned a project in the past, the banker will find out. As with equity investors, experience of the industry sector is a prerequisite, and the banker will closely review the business plan. The corporate structure and the strength and culture of its investors will be a major consideration.

If the financing falters, the banker will hope that his original investigation into the borrower's character allowed him to form an accurate judgement; in difficult situations, the experience and skill of the banker and the borrower's integrity are tested to extremes.

The business operation must be managed in such a way that, if problems occur, the management is prepared to discuss plans for recovery with the bank at an early stage – the raft of financial covenants in the loan agreement will serve as a reminder to do this. In addition to testing the assumptions underlying the recovery plan and discussing alternatives, the bank, in these circumstances, will have to be completely convinced that the original character judgement was correct and will remain so throughout a difficult period. The strength and support of the shareholders will need to be apparent, because the banker will have to convince his Credit Committee that it is sensible to continue to support the business.

Amount

A favourite question is: "What is the most that you will lend me?" Once the borrower has established this, then the desk-top value of assets usually rise, and the cash-flow projections increase to a level which then compares favourably with the magnitude of the loan required. However, the question of amount should be tackled in a different way. First of all, the borrower should assume that they will have to put some cash into the cost of the acquisition; as a starting point, assume that the amount of the equity investment plus subordinated debt will need to match the level of bank debt required. However, there really is no little black book or formula that dictates lending policy, and having taken into account management's stake and the level of debt required, the banker will focus very clearly on cash flow and ability to service costs from revenues. The banker will also look at the asset value of the business.

Maturity

The borrower will want the financing to be as long-term as possible, with no prepayment fee, allowing the company to take advantage of peaks in the market, or to gear up on increased value which may be used in the next project and to expand the business. The banker, on the other hand, will want to restrict the term of the loan, and would also like to have a fee if it is prepaid. So how is a compromise reached? The banker examines the business plan (cash-flow projection), and assesses the margin of safety. The banker will not accept exposure on high anticipated residual values for the business's assets, or optimistic growth projections, unless he is financing on a basis other than straight forward bank debt.

Purpose

The bank will need to be convinced that the entire transaction has been fully evaluated and is soundly based. If the borrowers are purchasing a business in a sector in which they have no previous experience, then they must expect to justify fully both their reasons and their ability. If they are investing in a business which is in a competitive market with over-capacity, then they will need to be especially persuasive. The banker will probably already have a view on the sector of the market, but will also want to investigate further. The technical operation, with particular emphasis on environmental risk, training and safety, will have to be of the highest quality. Environmental risk is now considered to be a real risk to both the owner of a business and the financier; concerns in respect of pollution risks and lender liability have recently caused heated debate during meetings of nervous credit committees.

Having established that the purpose of the loan is acceptable, and having formed an initial feeling for the proposition, the banker will turn his attention to the likely return for the risk. However, not until all aspects of the transaction have been evaluated will the pricing be settled.

Account

The borrower should expect to receive an account for the reward the banker requires, set against the risk that he perceives. The pricing should be a reflection of the perceived risk of the transaction, but is always subject to the bank's minimum margin or hurdle rate – the bank's cost of capital is high, and capital is in short supply. The longer the term, the higher the price. There will be an arrangement, or "front end" fee; this is important to the banker, as it helps to demonstrate internally some of the rewards to the bank of staying in this sector of the market.

Margins have moved upwards in corporate markets but, considering the risks that the banks take, the borrowers generally strike a fair deal; this becomes apparent when one compares the internal rate of return that the venture capitalist or mezzanine lender requires, compared to the bank's margin.

Repayment

The combination of the amount of the loan, the cash flow, and the term, dictates the ability of the business to cover operating expenses, interest and capital repayments. The overall gearing of the business will also be examined in some detail. If the cash-flow revenue does not contain a good margin of safety after operating costs, debt-servicing and sensitivity modelling, then the borrower may not be granted the loan. Interest-rate fluctuation can affect cash flow quite dramatically; the banker can offer a fixed-interest rate loan or a "cap and collar", so that this cost can be controlled.

If revenues are in foreign currencies, then the loan can contain a currency option. Multi-currency options have a place in the market, but not for speculation. Any company using a multi-currency loan to play the currency market is adding to its risks if it has no income in these currencies.

The bank, having satisfied itself that the structure of the financing against projected cash flow is reasonable, will now look at asset-value quality and other aspects affecting the available security package.

Insurance

In this context "Insurance" means the bank's protection against business failure, and the existence or otherwise of a security package. This is the banker's last resort if things go badly wrong with the financing, and the business cannot be sold as a going concern.

Financing highly leveraged businesses is risky. Bankers are requested to provide long-term funds in an uncertain marketplace. The ability of management to adapt to market changes caused by competition, economic forces or structural change, together with the safety margin allowed for in the cash flows, is far more important to the banker than a dubious security package.

Summary

Bankers will require a very thorough presentation based on the above, together with a regular information package which will enable the bank to monitor the exposure. Risk management is the skill that both the management team and the banker need to have to ride the roller-coaster of a volatile business environment successfully. A healthy cash-flow is all-important in a crisis situation, and the business should be financed and managed in such a way as to have reserves that will cushion against the unexpected.

Debt and risk-hedging products

Working capital facilities

These are the banking facilities which any business needs to support its normal activities; they include overdrafts, revolving money-market loans, acceptances, documentary credits, bonds and guarantees, negotiation and foreign exchange dealing lines. The buy-out provides an opportunity to review both the existing needs and the future requirements of the business, bearing in mind any projected increases in turnover. It may well be that increased or different facilities and arrangements will be appropriate after the buy-out. For example, overseas suppliers who had previously supplied the business on open-account terms, on the basis that it was part of a large and publicly quoted group, might decide to supply only on documentary-credit terms until the success of the buy-out is proven. In many cases, the business will have had access to group banking facilities that were negotiated by its parent company. After the buy-out, it may find that as an independent business the costs of the working capital facilities, and indeed money transmission services, rise.

Acquisition funding

Acquisition funding from a bank will usually take the form of a reducing term loan. The bank will fund this loan through borrowing from the money market. Interest on the loan will consequently be linked to Libor (London Inter Bank Offered Rate), which fluctuates according to changes in the interest rates available on the money market. Although the loan may be for a term of several years, in practice it will consist of a series of short-term advances which are rolled over at maturity. Draw-down periods for these advances of three, six and 12 months are typically permitted under the loan agreement. Libor will be fixed for the period of the advance, thus fixing the borrowing costs until the next roll-over.

For smaller loans, the interest rate applying to the loan may be linked to the bank's base rate, or the bank may be able to provide the loan at a fixed interest rate for part or all of the term.

A term of up to seven or eight years is typical for acquisition loans. Where there is little security for the bank, or there is perceived to be a relatively high level of uncertainty in the future cash flows, then a shorter term is likely to be required. Ideally, banks prefer to see the loan repaid in equal amounts each year. Nevertheless, it is often necessary for the early repayments to be at a reduced level, particularly if new capital investment or a rationalisation programme is a feature of the business plan. However, in the low inflation/low growth outlook of the 1990s, banks will need to be persuaded to agree a structure of increasing loan repayments, which can only be met if significant growth is achieved.

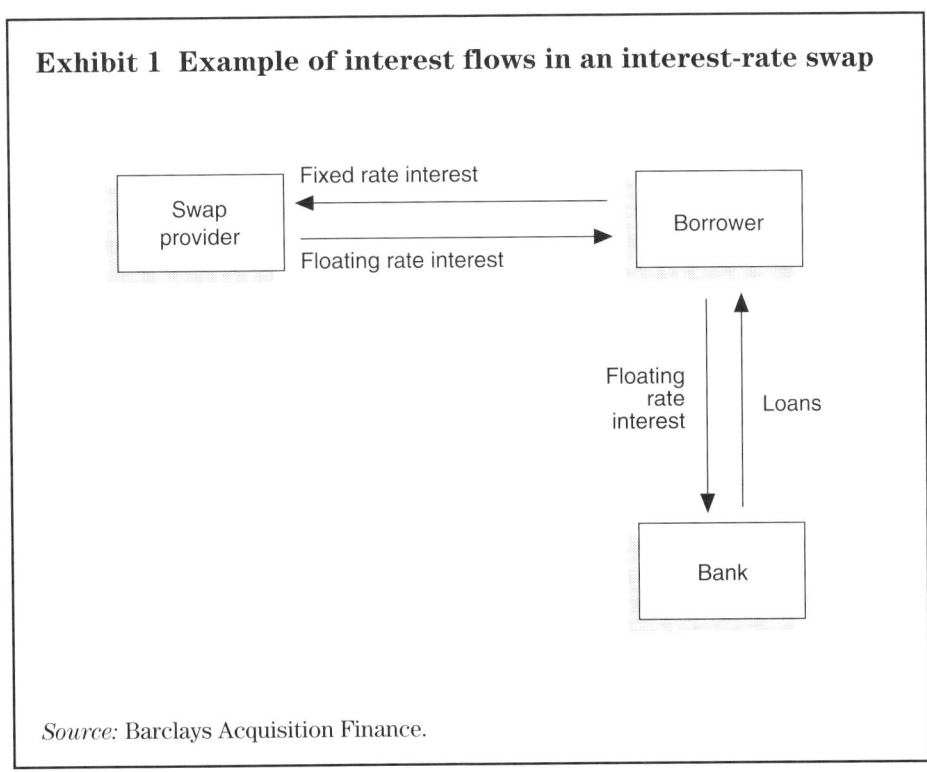

Exhibit 1 Example of interest flows in an interest-rate swap

Source: Barclays Acquisition Finance.

In some situations it may be possible for the term debt or part of the term debt to be structured as a commercial mortgage against the premises of the business and to be repayable over a longer term, perhaps up to 15 years or more.

Interest-rate exposure management
It is likely that the acquisition of the business will be partly funded through term borrowings which are subject to an interest rate linked to Libor, or to a base rate. In the case of buy-outs, a high level of gearing is common, as this will enhance the returns of the investors, and the financial results of the business are therefore likely to be sensitive to interest-rate movements. It is therefore usually prudent for the business to hedge against increases in interest rates. Banks have specialists who can advise on hedging strategies and methods – the techniques can be highly complex. The most common methods are listed and explained below.

Interest-rate swaps

An interest-rate swap enables companies to change the interest-rate structure of their borrowings, independently of the underlying borrowings. It is an agreement whereby one party pays a fixed interest rate at specified intervals over an agreed period, and the other pays a floating rate set for each of the intervals, calculated on a notional principal amount. It is agreed that all payments are to be made on a net basis that represents the difference between the fixed and floating rate. Exhibit 1 illustrates the interest flows in a situation in which a borrower has taken out a swap to fix his interest cost on a floating loan:

An interest-rate swap involves the borrower entering into a contractual arrangement under which the cost of closing out the contract early could be large, depending on how interest rates have moved since the contract was taken out, and the period to maturity. The provider of the swap will therefore treat these arrangements as credit exposures.

Interest-rate cap

By employing an interest-rate cap, the customer guarantees a rate at which funds can be borrowed; however, he is not committed to borrow at that cap rate, if the floating rate is lower. A cap is thus designed to give borrowers with rolling floating-rate borrowings, insurance against an increase in interest rates above a specified level (the cap rate), whilst retaining the ability to benefit from favourable Libor movements. A premium is generally payable by the customer at the outset. This premium is based on the level of the cap rate in relation to the floating rate and to the length of the period to be covered by the contract.

Foreign currency exposure management

Banks also provide advice and products to assist businesses in managing their foreign currency exposures. Foreign currency exposure management is a complex topic and is beyond the scope of this book. However, an example of the type of issue that can arise in a buy-out is where the vendor has had a policy of not hedging foreign currency receipts from overseas sales. The management team may decide that this is a risk that they prefer to manage. The bank will advise on the different methods of managing this exposure, for example, taking out forward exchange contracts to fix the sterling amount of the proceeds when the sale is agreed.

The buy-out may result in the creation of new foreign exchange exposures and opportunities to manage this exposure. For example, if the business has substantial net assets in a foreign country, then it may be appropriate for part of the acquisition loan to be partly drawn in the currency of that foreign country. The effect of this will be to create a foreign currency liability to match against the foreign currency asset, and so reduce the net exposure to that currency. This will help to reduce the effect on the consolidated balance sheet of the UK holding company of any fluctuations in the foreign currency exchange rate.

Specialist finance

Through their subsidiaries, banks can often provide various forms of specialist finance such as factoring, invoice discounting, leasing and hire purchase. These methods of borrowing may offer lower costs and higher percentage advances than a bank may be willing to provide. These forms of finance are usually based upon the lender financing specific assets or classes of assets, often with the lender having legal ownership of the asset. For example, factoring and invoicing are used to finance debtors and leasing and hire purchase to finance plant, machinery, cars and computers. The borrower will need to consider the accounting and taxation implications of these forms of finance before making a decision.

Where these forms of finance form part of an overall package of debt funding and a bank is providing committed term facilities, it will want assurances that these specialist forms of finance will not be cancelled at the first sign of trading difficulties. If this were to happen, then the bank might find its own facilities drawn down to repay the specialist lender and the business would run into cash-flow difficulties. Specialist finance providers are not always prepared to make a term commitment and so these forms of finance may not prove appropriate despite their advantages. Also, leasing and hire purchase are often only intended to finance the purchase of new assets and consequently may not be available to fund the acquisition.

Case study – the MBO of EngCo

"EngCo" is a specialist engineering company, based in the East Midlands, which manufactures high-precision valves. The valves are used in a wide range of industrial and commercial applications and are sold world-wide. About 40 per cent of sales are to the UK market, 20 per cent to Western Europe, 30 per cent to the USA and Canada and 10 per cent to the rest of the world. In Western Europe, the sales are through national distributors in each country. In North America, the sales are through a subsidiary sales company, based in the United States. The valves are technically superior to competing products and the business has a reputation for innovation and high quality.

EngCo is owned by "BigCo", a diversified manufacturing group listed on the Stock Exchange. BigCo is under some pressure to reduce its gearing and is intending to achieve this by disposing of its non-core operations including EngCo. BigCo has set the following disposal timetable:

Stage 1: Outline information provided to interested parties. Initial offers to be received by the Offer Date.

Stage 2: Access to detailed information provided to a shortlist of bidders. Revised offers, with evidence of financial backing, to be received by Offer Date plus two months.

Stage 3: Letter of intent to be entered into with successful bidder. Simultaneous exchange of contracts and completion by Offer Date plus three months.

Exhibit 2   The initial appraisal flow chart

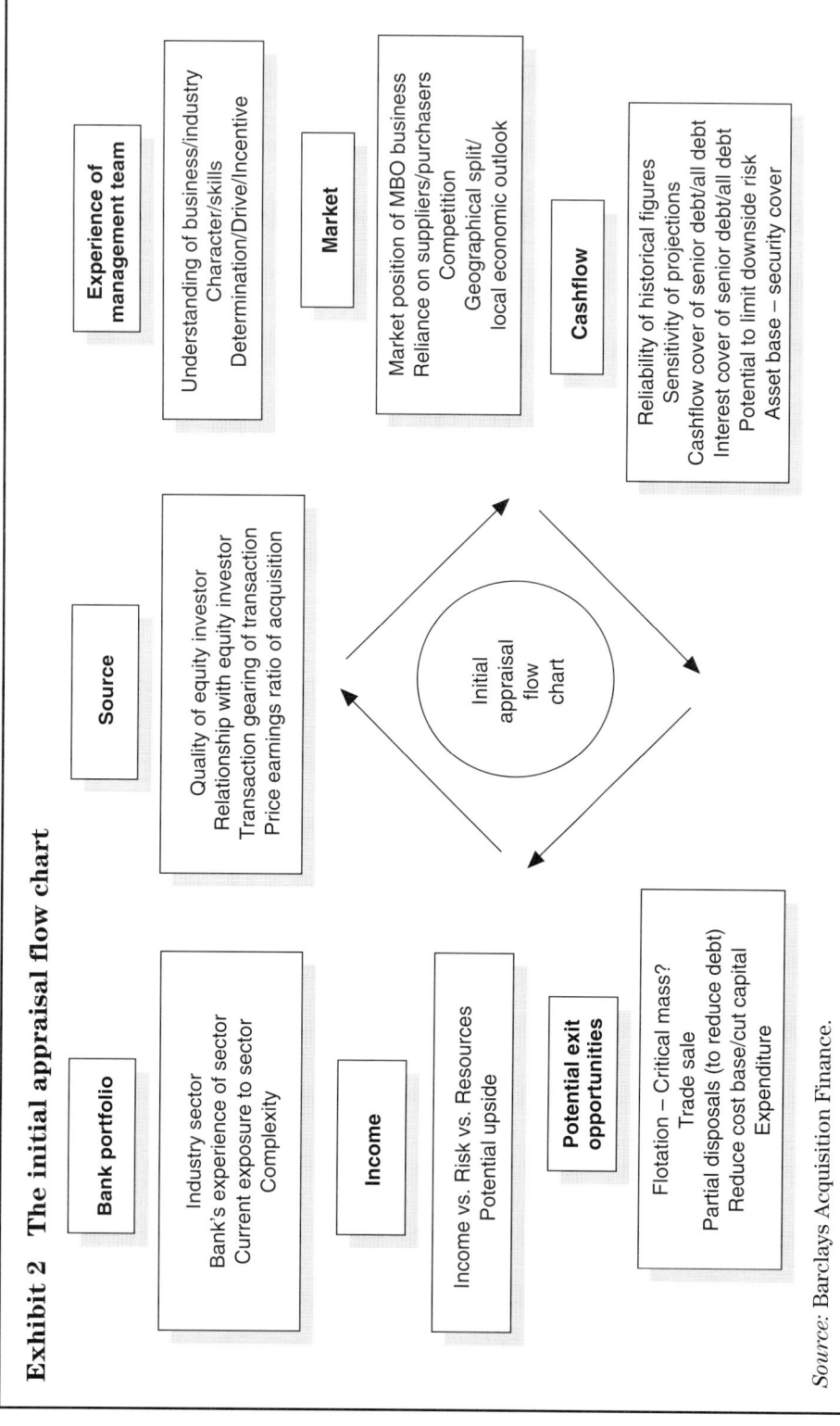

Experience of management team

Understanding of business/industry
Character/skills
Determination/Drive/Incentive

Market

Market position of MBO business
Reliance on suppliers/purchasers
Competition
Geographical split/
local economic outlook

Cashflow

Reliability of historical figures
Sensitivity of projections
Cashflow cover of senior debt/all debt
Interest cover of senior debt/all debt
Potential to limit downside risk
Asset base – security cover

Source

Quality of equity investor
Relationship with equity investor
Transaction gearing of transaction
Price earnings ratio of acquisition

Initial
appraisal
flow
chart

Bank portfolio

Industry sector
Bank's experience of sector
Current exposure to sector
Complexity

Income

Income vs. Risk vs. Resources
Potential upside

Potential exit opportunities

Flotation – Critical mass?
Trade sale
Partial disposals (to reduce debt)
Reduce cost base/cut capital
Expenditure

Source: Barclays Acquisition Finance.

The initial approach to Money Bank is made by Bee, Count & Terse – the firm of accountants advising the management team. They advise Money Bank that the management team has made an initial offer of £15 million, and has passed through to Stage 2. The management intend to fund the acquisition with a 50:50 split of debt:equity. Money Bank is asked by Bee, Count & Terse to quickly confirm whether it is interested or not in pursuing the opportunity. A detailed business plan is provided to Money Bank. Money Bank's reaction to this request is to undertake an initial appraisal of the attractiveness of the proposal, using the Initial Appraisal Flowchart (Exhibit 2) as the structure for their analysis. At this stage, in order to provide a quick response, it is necessary for a lot of the information to be taken at face value, although it will be rigorously tested at a later stage.

The management team
The management team will have a critical influence on the success of the MBO. Money Bank will therefore want to be satisfied at an early stage of the capabilities, integrity and commitment of the management team. Money Bank will form its views over the period of the MBO process, but will certainly expect to form a favourable initial judgement.

In the case of EngCo, the management team comprises the existing senior management of the business: the managing director, finance controller, marketing director and operations director. Their *curricula vitae* confirm that they have extensive experience of the industry and have been with EngCo for a number of years, during which time the business has successfully expanded.

The arrangement of borrowing facilities, pension and tax matters are handled direct by the Head Office of BigCo. The finance controller will, therefore, take on wider responsibilities after the buy-out, when he becomes finance director. The finance controller of EngCo is relatively young, but he has an impressive track record, and Money Bank is able to satisfy itself that he will quickly be able to adjust to the greater responsibilities that the role of finance director of an independent business will involve. As the transaction progresses, Money Bank refines its initial assessment of the management team by obtaining personal references about them, and by observing the performance of the team during the MBO process.

The sponsors/advisers
Money Bank will prefer the management team to be backed by an established equity provider, and will take considerable comfort from the presence of advisers with proven track records in the buy-out market. With the support of experienced sponsors/advisers, the management team is less likely to over-pay for the business, and will be better placed to negotiate favourable terms. Also, with experienced sponsors/advisers, the process is more likely to run smoothly and without too many crises.

The management team of EngCo is being advised by the Birmingham office of Bee, Count & Terse, a major firm of accountants, and they have appointed Nether, End & Scribble, a large firm of Birmingham solicitors, as their legal advisers. Both firms are active and experienced as buy-out advisers.

The management team have not yet selected the institutional equity investor, but have narrowed the choice down to two equity houses, both of whom are well known to Money Bank through a number of previous transactions. From its experience of these equity houses, Money Bank knows that they adopt a professional approach to due diligence investigations and are skilful negotiators; it is confident that, even if the business should falter following the buy-out, the equity houses will be likely to maintain a supportive stance, including injecting additional funds should this prove necessary.

The business

Money Bank will primarily be lending against the future cash flows of the business. The security value of the business is a secondary consideration, and Money Bank will therefore focus on the stability of the cash flow. Where cash flow is uncertain or is subject to large fluctuations, then the acquisition is probably best funded by equity capital, with perhaps a modest level of working capital from the bank. The industrial/services sector that the business operates in will usually provide a good indication of the stability of the cash flow. For example, whereas the capital goods sector tends to be highly cyclical, the food retailing sector tends to be relatively stable.

In the case of EngCo, although demand for its product is affected by the level of economic activity, the wide spread of industrial and commercial applications for its valves, and the diversified nature of its international markets, results in the demand for its products being reasonably stable. This is evidenced by its financial results through the last two recessions. Money Bank also checks to ensure that the business is not over-reliant on any one supplier or customer.

Financial projections

Money Bank will want to ensure that the projected cash flows are sufficient to service the debt and provide an adequate buffer against any likely degree of under-performance.

The projections for EngCo show continuing growth and steadily rising profits. The assumptions underlying this growth are in line with the results achieved in previous years. Money Bank's initial assessment is that the projections appear a little ambitious, but even at a more conservative rate of growth the debt can be comfortably serviced. As more information becomes available, Money Bank will confirm that each of the principal assumptions are realistic and will sensitise the projections to show the effect on the ability to service debt of an under performance of the business. The amount by which the projections are sensitised will depend upon the certainty of the underlying assumptions and the historical fluctuations seen in the business.

Alternative sources of repayment

In the event that the actual cash flow falls short of the projected levels, and the borrowings cannot be fully serviced, Money Bank will wish to have a fall back source of repayment. Money Bank will therefore evaluate the potential exit opportunities for its lending, which might take the form of a complete disposal of the business, either through a stock market flotation or trade sale; a partial disposal of the business or assets; or a reduction in costs and capital expenditure to improve the cash flow.

EngCo is probably too small to achieve a flotation. However, there are several serious trade buyers who are known to be bidding against the management team and Money Bank conclude that a trade sale would be a realistic option. An alternative would be for EngCo to cut the large research and development and capital expenditure programmes. This action would significantly improve the short term cash flow, but in the longer term would be to the detriment of the business.

Internal considerations

In determining its attitude to a lending opportunity, a bank will also consider the financing proposal in the context of its own risk versus return versus resource criteria and portfolio considerations. For example, a bank may wish to avoid increasing its exposure to a particular industry sector because of an already high level of exposure to that sector.

After completing its initial appraisal, a bank will form a judgement on the proposal. Sometimes the conclusion will be that the proposal as presented is a realistic banking proposition, subject to the initial appraisal being confirmed. On other occasions the conclusion will be that there are major weaknesses in the proposal and there is no point in continuing discussions. However, in many cases

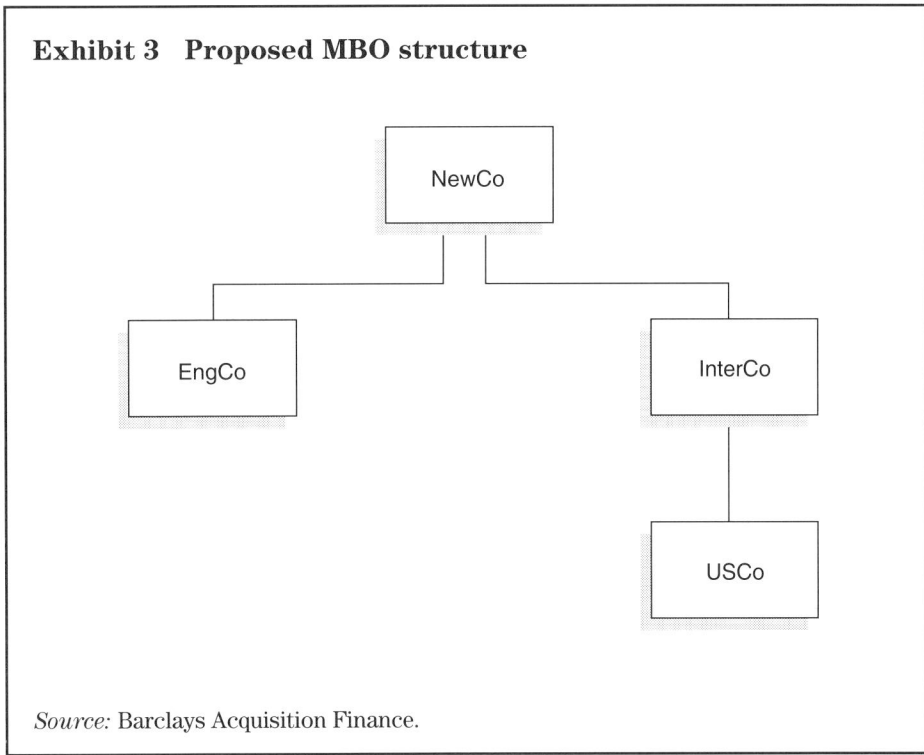

Exhibit 3 Proposed MBO structure

Source: Barclays Acquisition Finance.

the conclusion will be that potentially the transaction is bankable, but that the proposed structure is not acceptable; for example, a greater proportion of equity funding may be required.

Money Bank, having now completed its initial assessment and having satisfied itself that the EngCo buy-out opportunity is a realistic banking proposal, confirms to Bee, Count & Terse that it is keen to continue working on the transaction. Bee, Count & Terse request that Money Bank obtain credit approval to issue outline terms for providing both a loan to help fund the acquisition and working capital facilities for normal trading purposes. The outline terms are to be attached to the revised offer to BigCo in order to provide evidence of financial backing.

In this case study, the management team of EngCo have already made considerable progress in the MBO process. However, in many cases the management team will approach the bank at a much earlier stage, possibly when the MBO is only an idea. This is often beneficial for both the management team and the bank. The bank will be in a position to respond more quickly when a decision is required because it has been involved from an early stage, whilst the management team will be able to take account of the bank's views from the beginning.

Detailed appraisal

Before issuing outline terms, Money Bank will undertake a thorough review of the EngCo business to confirm its initial appraisal. The review will include:

– visits to the main operations of the business;
– meeting all the senior management team and the second tier of management;
– in-depth analysis of the historic trading results and financial projections;
– review of the prospects for the products of the business and its competitive position, and
– review of the reliance on, and relationship with, the vendor, suppliers, customers and the financial soundness of those major trading partners.

In the case of MBO transactions the bank (and usually the institutional investor) will require the provision of "expert" reports. These will typically include an independent accountants report on the business and a property valuation. Reports on the market and environmental issues are also often required. These may be available before the outline terms are issued, but if not they will be listed as conditions precedent. In the case of EngCo, the management team, the institutional investor and Money Bank agree that these reports will only be obtained after the letter of intent has been signed with BigCo. Completion is to be within one month of the letter of intent being signed and as a result the timetable for completion and review of these reports will be tight. At this stage, Money Bank will also consider in detail the structure of the banking facilities and the security. This will form part of a wider review of the structure of the transaction and the structure of the funding and taxation matters.

Structure

For the MBO of EngCo it is proposed that "NewCo", a newly established company, acquires EngCo. The management and equity investors will hold the shares in NewCo. The US sales company is a subsidiary of another BigCo group company and acts as the North American sales company for the products of other BigCo group companies. As a result, only the relevant assets of the US sales company and not the company itself are to be sold. The assets consist of debtors, stocks, fixtures and fittings. A newly established US company ("USCo") is to acquire the assets. USCo will be owned by a UK-domiciled intermediate holding company, "InterCo", which will also be used as the immediate holding company for any future overseas subsidiaries that are established.

The proposed funding structure of the MBO of EngCo is straightforward – a 50:50 split between equity and bank debt. In more complex transactions, there can be mezzanine debt (debt with a repayment and security position that is subordinated to the bank debt), a vendor loan or deferred consideration. In these cases, the bank will carefully review the rights of each of the parties funding the acquisition. As a general rule, because the bank's potential returns will usually be limited to fixed fees and a margin, with no equity interest, it will expect its debt funding to rank in priority to the other sources of funds.

Having reviewed the structure of the transaction and funding, Money Bank will consider how the banking facilities and security package are best structured. With EngCo, Money Bank is being asked to help fund the acquisition cost with a 7.5 million term loan and to provide working capital facilities.

Acquisition loan

The history of stable cash flows and the presence of significant tangible assets enable a seven-year repayment term to be agreed for EngCo. In the first year following the buy-out, the management propose to invest in a major piece of equipment, which will enable significant cost reductions to be achieved and quicker turn-around of orders. To allow for this large cash outflow a reduced repayment instalment is agreed for the first year.

Money bank suggests to the management team that they should consider borrowing part of the loan through USCo in US dollars. After obtaining expert advice on the tax and legal implications, it is agreed that £7 million of the £7.5 million loan will be lent to NewCo in sterling and the balance to USCo in US dollars. This structure has a number of advantages, including:

– The interest charge on the US dollar loan will reduce both the taxable profits of USCo and the amount of funds it will need to upstream to NewCo to assist with the servicing of the UK borrowings.
– At the time of the buy-out interest rates are lower for US dollar borrowings than for sterling borrowings.
– Money Bank is able to improve its security position by taking security from USCo to secure the borrowings of USCo. Money Bank is more likely to be able to successfully enforce the security given by USCo if the proceeds are to be used to repay the direct borrowings of USCo than if they are to be used to repay

the borrowings of another company in a foreign country.

– The creation of a US dollar liability, which can be matched against the US dollar assets of USCo, and the creation of a US dollar interest charge, which can be matched against the US dollar profit stream, will assist NewCo in the management of its foreign exchange exposure.

The possibility of increases in interest rates is identified by both the management team and Money Bank as a major risk. Money Bank therefore arrange for specialists from the bank's Derivatives Department to make a presentation to the management, detailing interest-rate management strategies and products. The management team decide to hedge 75 per cent of the loan by the purchase of an interest-rate cap and arrangements are made by Money Bank for the cap to be purchased on completion.

Working-capital facilities

EngCo requires an overdraft facility to absorb the peaks in its cash flow – for example, at the end of each month when the salaries are paid.

In addition, EngCo requires:

– a foreign exchange dealing line;
– a duty deferment bond;
– a documentary credit facility (in connection with the supply of certain components from the Far East); and
– a Bankers Automated Clearing Services (BACS) limit to enable electronic payment of salaries and UK suppliers.

The foreign exchange dealing line is required to assist EngCo in the hedging of its foreign currency exposure. It is EngCo's practice to take out forward contracts to fix the sterling cost/proceeds of foreign currency purchases/sales. Money Bank suggests to the management team that as there are some foreign currencies where there are regular receipts and payments, then it may be more cost-effective for EngCo to open foreign currency accounts with which to credit/debit transactions in the relevant currencies rather than convert to/from sterling every time there is a foreign currency transaction.

Security

Money Bank will be making a substantial and long term lending commitment to NewCo, and the only certainty is that the actual trading results will be different from those projected in the business plan. Money Bank therefore specifies in the Outline Terms that it requires a full security package consisting of first fixed and floating charges over all the UK assets and cross guarantees from NewCo and its subsidiaries. Similar security, as far as is legally possible under local law, is to be given by USCo.

Covenants

In addition to requiring a full security package, Money Bank includes a number of financial covenants in the Outline Terms. These are intended to act as an early warning of potential financial difficulties and to prompt the management team to take action to address the underlying problems. A breach of the financial covenants will constitute an event of default and will thus give Money Bank a right to take a number of actions, including making a demand for repayment. The covenants specified are:

– Profit before interest and tax: Interest
– Cash flow before interest and loan repayments: Interest and loan repayments
– Borrowings: Profit before interest and tax
– Minimum net worth

The first two covenants are measures of the ability of the business to service its financial obligations. One method of valuing a business is to apply an appropriate price-earnings ratio to its earnings. The third covenant thus indirectly relates the level of borrowings to the value of the business. The final covenant acts as a trigger against any reduction in the net worth of the business that might not be caught by the other covenants.

Having satisfied itself on the points discussed above and having obtained internal credit approval, Money Bank issues Outline Terms to the management team. The revised offer submitted by the management team is successful and a letter of intent is signed with BigCo.

Count-down to completion

Instructions are given by Money Bank, in conjunction with the investing equity institution, for the accountants report and property valuation to be prepared. An environmental report is also commissioned. EngCo's products and production process have no adverse environmental implications. However, one of the factory sites has been used for a variety of industrial uses since the 1930s; there is, therefore, a risk of site contamination from a previous use. The report identifies a number of problems, but all are minor and require no clean-up operations. Money Bank instructs its solicitors to draft the facilities agreement and security documents and, after two or three drafts, final copies are agreed by Money Bank and the management team.

Money Bank reviews the principal transaction documents, including the Sale and Purchase Agreements for EngCo and the American assets, the investment agreement between the management team and the equity house and the service contracts of the management team. In reviewing the Sale and Purchase Agreement, Money Bank checks that it reflects the commercial agreement that has been agreed with BigCo and that adequate protection for NewCo is incorporated in the agreement in the form of warranties and indemnities, restrictive covenants and conditions precedent and subsequent. As completion day approaches, activity becomes frenetic: negotiations continue to agree the outstanding issues and the reporting accountants and the environmental consultants first make oral presentations of their main conclusions before submitting draft reports and, finally, signed reports. Given the tight timetable, it is essential for the management team, the equity house, and Money Bank to have as much notice as possible of any significant problems to allow time for further investigations, or for more negotiations with the vendor. Finally, completion day arrives, agreement is reached on the outstanding points and the documents are amended and signed.

Money Bank has already opened bank accounts for NewCo and has made arrangements with the existing bankers of EngCo for the transfer of the banking business of the MBO business to Money Bank. The day-to-day banking business of EngCo thus continues with minimal interruption. After the buy-out has been completed, Money Bank monitors the progress of NewCo through the receipt of regular management information, and by making visits to the business.

Syndication

In the case of large transactions, the bank may ask a number of other banks to jointly provide the debt facilities, either by syndicating the debt after completion, or by arranging for a number of banks to commit before completion to participate in the debt. In the latter case, the banks will be known as Underwriting banks, and following completion may either retain the full amount of the debt or may syndicate the debt to further banks. Where the debt is syndicated in this way, then the principal bank will be known as the Arranger, and will negotiate on behalf of all the other banks. Following completion, a bank will be appointed as Agent for the syndicate of banks, and will act as the main point of contact between the bank and the borrower. The Arranger is often, though not always, appointed as Agent. Money Bank is happy to provide the full amount of the banking facilities for the MBO of EngCo itself and consequently there is no syndication of the bank debt.

Due diligence - the role of the reporting accountant

Once an agreement has been reached in principle between the various parties involved in a management buy-out, the financing institutions will wish to carry out "due diligence" enquiries. Up until this point, the decision to finance the buy-out has been based largely on information supplied by, and representations made by, the management team. It is likely that the financial adviser to the buy-out team will not have conducted an independent review, but will also have relied on the management's representations. However, any indicative offers of finance will be subject to detailed due diligence, which will seek to verify the information provided. The due diligence process is particularly important for the financiers, as only limited warranties and indemnities are likely to be forthcoming from the vendor.

Scope

The exact scope of the due diligence enquiries will depend on a number of factors, including:

– the complexity and diversity of the target business;
– the familiarity of the investors with the industry and market in which the business operates; and
– the investors' identification of particular areas of risk based on their initial enquiries and a review of the management team's business plan.

Due diligence enquiries may include an independent market survey carried out by experienced marketing consultants or industry experts, particularly if the investors are unfamiliar with the industry or if the management's revenue projections seem too optimistic.

Investors will also seek independent assurances on the background and experience of the management team. They will take up a number of references on each member of the team; they will also consult any contacts that they have within the industry at a senior level as well as the firm's major customers and leading suppliers.

The most detailed due diligence carried out by the financiers will be to commission a wide-ranging report from a firm of accountants. The scope of the report is usually determined by the lead investor in consultation with other investors, lenders and the management team; it is unlikely to include a formal audit. The report should be focused on areas of particular concern that have been identified by the investors. Such areas might include the gross margins earned on different products, the evaluation of stock and work in progress, capital expenditure programmes, or the sensitivity of cash-flow projections to fluctuations in the level of revenues. Detailed planning at the outset of the investigation should ensure that there is no duplication of the work to be carried out by legal advisors, or of due diligence already conducted, or to be conducted, by the financiers.

The scope of the report should be agreed in advance by all parties financing the buy-out, so that separate or additional reports are not required by mezzanine financiers or providers of bank finance, who may have different areas of concern or different requirements for the verification of information to those of the equity provider. For example, a provider of bank finance will be particularly interested in interest cover, gearing levels, asset backing and the effect of a detailed sensitivity analysis on these ratios.

The report should give the reader a thorough understanding of the business, including any potential problem areas, so that a balanced decision may be taken regarding the proposed investment. Often the reporting accountants will seek to identify the strengths, weaknesses, opportunities and threats relating to the business and to identify and evaluate the critical success factors of the business. A typical report on a medium-sized company will be in the region of 100 pages and could have up to 30 or 40 appendices. The due diligence exercise will place an additional burden on the management team at a time when they are also involved in the drafting of a large number of legal documents connected with the management buy-out as well as running the business on a day-to-day basis. However, it is crucial that appropriate time and attention is given to the due diligence exercise, as its completion will be a key condition of funding a management buy-out. The leader of the buy-out team may consider it necessary to delegate the task of liaison with the investigating accountants to one member of the team, whilst another deals with running the business. This can ease pressure on the team, but the accountants will nevertheless need to interview each member of the team at some stage during their work.

Detailed contents

An accountants' due diligence report for a management buy-out will require an accountant not only to examine the history and current position of a business, and its financial track record, but also to comment constructively on the projected financial performance of the management buy-out vehicle. A reporting accountant is required to provide a rigorous analysis of, and commentary on, many aspects of the business. This task may be made more complicated if the management buy-out companies are situated in a number of countries – although leading firms of accountants, with their sophisticated international networks, are usually well-placed to contribute expert local knowledge in each location.

The due diligence for a management buy-out is very different from a standard pre-acquisition investigation on behalf of an acquiror. Usually, one of the principal purposes of such investigations is to obtain sufficient ammunition to negotiate a reduction in an agreed purchase price. Due diligence for a management buy-out is, in part a confirmatory exercise and is intended to provide comfort as to the accuracy of information and financial data already provided to the financiers; it is also intended to provide informed professional advice and commentary on the financial projections and the proposed structure of the management buy-out vehicle. A wide range of taxation issues will need to be considered – tax considerations sometimes prove to be the driving force behind the way in which an investment is structured.

In the past, financiers have often complained that due diligence reports have included too much factual information, with too little comment or analysis of key issues. An accountant preparing a due diligence report must be prepared to make commercial judgements. It is ironic that, whilst the accountant with a wide range of professional experience involving a number of different businesses and transactions is best-placed to provide such advice and commentary, the most common complaint levelled at such reports is that they tend to be bland and lacking an informed and incisive commentary. The lead investor should be able to recommend investigating accountants who will have the necessary experience to prepare an effective due diligence report.

The principal areas that an investigating accountant will be asked to examine are discussed in turn in the following sections.

Background

This section will provide an evaluation of the operational infrastructure of the business. It will describe:

– the history of the company,
– the ownership of the company,
– the organisation of the company,
– the staffing of the company, and
– the company premises.

The business

This section will describe what the business does, how it operates, and where it makes its profit. The description is likely to include a review of the company's products and margins, selling methods, marketing strategy, customer base, production methods and suppliers. The accountant may also be required to review the market within which the business operates. This review will cover:

– past performance and anticipated growth levels,
– competition facing the company,
– the comparative position of the company and its products, and
– the research and development programme.

Management information systems

In the report, particular emphasis will be paid to the accountants' assessment of the quality of the management information systems, and the accounting controls within the business.

Financial history

The accountants will review the historical results of the business to ensure that these support any projected profit trends. They will be required to explain what has happened to the company during the last three to five years and to identify any changes in accounting policy to ensure that the track record has been prepared on a consistent basis and in accordance with generally accepted accounting principles.

The accountants will need to make any adjustments that are necessary to reflect the historical record of the business as if it had been an independent entity. This may include substituting inter-group charges for services – for example, insurance costs or computer processing supplied by the parent company – with arms-length charges for those services as if they had been supplied by third parties. Equally, the business may have suffered management charges from its parent company which will not be incurred in the future.

The most contentious area of this section is often the identification of exceptional costs that the management consider were incurred at the behest of the parent company, or for wider group purposes, and which should therefore be identified separately in the company's track record.

Recent balance sheet

This section will provide an analysis of the balance sheet of the company on the latest available date, to ensure that it provides a fair reflection of the net assets of the business.

Working capital

The financiers will require the investigating accountant to comment on the cash flows of the business during the last three to five years, in order to identify the normal cash-flow cycle of the business.

Taxation

A review will be required of the current and deferred corporation tax that is liable to be levied on the company and of any exposure to VAT and PAYE liabilities that have not been provided in the financial statements together with an overall comment on the company's standard of compliance with statutory requirements.

Financial projections

An examination of the company's financial projections for the next three to five years, covering both the profit projections and the forecast working capital requirements, is a critical area of due diligence. The accountants will be required to provide a detailed commentary on the assumptions and accounting bases underlying the financial projections, together with a robust sensitivity analysis.

Management

The accountants will be asked to provide an assessment of the management team. This part of the report may be communicated verbally rather than in writing, and it is unlikely that management will be made aware of these comments.

Management buy-out issues

This section will assess the impact on the business of its being separated from the parent company. It will include an analysis of those services currently provided by the parent that will need to be obtained from third parties after the management buy-out, and an analysis of any costs imposed by the parent company which will not recur in the future.

This section of the report usually discusses pension arrangements, but other areas that may be affected by the buy-out include: personnel services, insurance arrangements, company secretarial services, treasury management and management information and accounting systems. The investigating accountants will be required to assess the quality of the management's plans to obtain the relevant support, and to confirm the likely cost of such services by reference to quotations from third parties obtained by the management team.

Adding value

The importance of an informative, analytical and timely due diligence report by the accountants, which gives clear, unambiguous opinions, has been stressed above. The key areas and issues on which the accountant's wide professional experience may be expected to provide "added value" are set out below.

Commentary on assumptions

The projections of the future profit and loss accounts and cash flows of the business are of major importance in the financiers' decision-making process. Although accountants cannot be expected to confirm that, in their opinion, a forecast is capable of being achieved, there is a requirement for a detailed, analytical commentary. The assumptions made in the forecast should be compared to results that have been achieved historically, or to those that have been achieved elsewhere in the industry. The assumptions should be vigorously challenged through discussion with all members of the management team, and any areas of concern or doubt should be brought to the attention of the financiers.

Sensitivity analysis

The examination of the assumptions underlying the financial projections will highlight any variables to which the business is particularly vulnerable. A detailed sensitivity analysis, applied to the profit and cash-flow projections, will outline the effect of any negative changes in these variables. The accountants should be in a position, following this review, to suggest the levels of contingency that the financiers will need if there is a shortfall in the projections. This is particularly important, given the leveraged nature of many management buy-outs, in respect of the cash-flow projections. It is obviously unfortunate if the buy-out team are obliged to return to the financiers after only a short period of time because over-optimistic projections have proved invalid, and they need to raise additional finance. Again it is important that the accountants express a firm opinion as precisely as possible.

Management information systems

Constructive comments on the quality of management information systems, particularly management accounting and forecasting systems, can prove invaluable. This is especially true in the early days of a management buy-out, when the management team must retain close control over the business whilst coming to terms with an unfamiliar level of independence. The accountants' report should not only highlight the weaknesses, if any, of the existing system, but also provide an immediate action plan to enable management to address the most pressing issues. The preparation of a medium-term plan to enhance the systems – which may be monitored by non-executive members of the Board – adds value to the accountants' work.

Financial structure

The financial structure of a management buy-out may change significantly during the period of negotiation. The accountants' report provides an opportunity for the interest and dividend payments and loan and preference share redemption profile of the financing structure to be set against the company's cash-flow projection. The analysis of the sensitivity of the financial structure of the management buy-out is of prime importance.

The management team and the financiers are sometimes reluctant to look for an investment of more than the minimum cash requirement to purchase the company and to provide working capital for the business. Understandably, the management wish to give up the minimum amount of equity to the financiers; the financiers tend to agree because they wish to protect their required rate of return, whilst satisfying the management's equity ambitions. A disinterested third party is often able to identify potential shortfalls in the cash position as originally envisaged, and this may result in a change to the deal structure. The accountants may also advise on interest rate management and hedging techniques in order to minimise the financial risk in the management buy-out vehicle. The accountants should also ensure that the company will be able to function effectively without being constantly in danger of breaching its bank covenants.

Fees and timescale

The cost of the accountants' due diligence report is typically met by the management buy-out vehicle. In addition to obtaining an estimate of the costs at the outset of the work, the management team should reach a clear agreement as to who shall bear the costs of the report if the transaction does not proceed. It is unlikely that the accountants' will be prepared to make the fees totally contingent upon the successful completion of the buy-out, although a reduced fee in the event of failure may be negotiated. Certainly, the accountants should remain completely independent of the success of the transaction so that this work can be carried out effectively. It is possible that the financiers, or indeed the vendor, may underwrite some element of the fees. It is crucial that the management team should be clear about the extent of their personal liability.

The cost of the report will depend on the time spent in its preparation, as accountants tend to charge on an hourly basis – and so will largely reflect the complexity of the business being examined. The fees for a report on a medium-sized company will typically range from £20,000 to £50,000. On average, the report will take from two to six weeks to prepare. A timetable should be agreed in advance to ensure that the report is delivered in a timely manner and does not hold up the transaction.

Conclusion

The accountants' due diligence report may be regarded as a necessary evil in order for the financiers to confirm the representations that have been made to them by the vendor and the management team during the negotiation of the management buy-out. However, it is also an opportunity for commercially minded accountants to bring their professional experience and insight to a transaction, and to add value through an analytical and constructive report.

6

Tax considerations

This chapter offers a brief discussion of the taxation issues that arise out of a management buy-out.[1] It does so from the perspective of the management, the acquisition vehicle (Newco), the target (Target) and, to a more limited extent, the vendor. The issues are outlined below and then discussed more fully in the following chapter sections.

The management side of the transaction will be most concerned with:

– interest relief on any borrowings that they have to make in order to invest in Newco;
– avoiding income tax charges on any increases in value in the shares that they own;
– an extraction of their income entitlement that is efficient with regard to tax and national insurance;
– capital gains and inheritance tax planning.

As far as Newco is concerned, the position with regard to tax needs to be considered quite carefully:

– Should it acquire a company, or assets and an undertaking?
– Will it be an investment or trading company for tax purposes?
– Can it be certain of tax relief for the interest on the borrowings used to effect the acquisition?
– Should tax clearance be obtained in respect of the acquisition?
– Should it effect a VAT grouping with Target?

[1] Of course, it is not possible to cover here all the taxation issues which may arise, or to treat the issues which are covered in great depth. In any event, the parties must always seek specific professional advice.

– Will there be a deduction for all or part of its acquisition costs?

– What will be the stamp duty cost of the acquisition, and is this mitigable?

– Will it have sufficient capacity to utilise advance corporation tax on the dividends that it pays?

Given that the shares in the Target are to be acquired, not much can be done to influence its tax position.

However, there are still matters to be considered:

– If Target has been loss making, is the vendor taking losses by way of group relief?

– Will there be (or has there been) a major change in the nature or conduct of the trade such that any pre-acquisition trading losses and surplus advance corporation tax may not be carried forward and any post-acquisition surplus advance corporation tax may not be carried back?

– If Target has made losses, should capital allowances be disclaimed?

– Are Target's tax affairs in order and up to date?

– Is the vendor considering a pre-sale dividend with or without advance corporation tax?

– What are the tax base values of Target's assets (particularly if any are to be realised)?

– Has Target had any capital-gains type assets transferred to it from other members of the group in the last six years?

The vendor will be seeking to minimise any tax liability:

– Should there be a pre-sale dividend?

– If a capital gain will arise, should Target be transferred intra group to a "capital loss" or "management expense" company?

– If amounts due from Target will not be fully recovered on the sale, will there be tax relief on the shortfall?

– What position should be adopted in the case of a request for tax warranties and indemnities?

Management

Interest relief

The basic rule for relief is that there must be an acquisition of shares in, or a loan to, an unquoted close company (of a defined type) by an individual who will own more than five per cent of the ordinary share capital, or who will work the greater part of his time in the actual management or conduct of the company (or an associated company).

The borrowing must give rise to "annual" rather than "short" interest and thus overdrafts (and credit card borrowings!) are disqualified. The interest must be "chargeable" under Case III of Schedule D – but this should always be the case for a UK tax resident individual borrower, even if the lender is not UK tax resident. If the lender is non-UK tax resident, care is needed as there will be an obligation to deduct and account for basic rate income tax when paying the interest – unless a relevant double-tax treaty can be invoked on a claim that is being made in advance.

The definition of a "close company" is lengthy and complex. Broadly, a company is close if it is "controlled" by five or fewer "participators", but non-close company participators are normally excluded. Holdings of "associates" have to be aggregated when determining whether five or fewer participators are in control. Control will usually be found to rest with the managers alone before the shareholdings of the financial backers are taken into account. However, in many cases, control will lie with the backers once their investment has been made – rendering the company "unclose". This is an intensely practical problem and the classic solution has been for the managers to invest first, as relief for interest continues after a company ceases to be close, provided that all other conditions are met. However, there have been problems with this approach; these have been caused by the status of Newco at the time that the managers invest.

For relief to be available, Newco must be a company which exists wholly or mainly for the purpose of carrying on a trade on a commercial basis, or holding shares in, or making loans to, such a company or companies which it, Newco, controls. There are other qualifying purposes, but this definition is the one that is generally appropriate to buy-outs. Until recently, it was assumed by many buy-out teams that Newco's recorded intentions were sufficient to satisfy this test, and that the company would not have to own anything at the time of the managers' subscription – though it must have a source of income in order to qualify as being in a tax accounting period. All appeared to be well, until the Inland Revenue took a case to the Commissioners and then to the High Court. The Revenue lost and, at the time of writing, it is understood that the decision has become final.

An alternative relief may be available for interest on borrowings that are used to acquire shares in what becomes an employee-controlled company. In practice, the relief outlined above is the one that is usually relied on; the alternative relief will not be considered further here.

On occasion, a manager may wish to invest in Newco through the medium of his own investment company. This is comparatively rare, as it brings with it the possibility of two tiers of taxation: one on a sale of shares in Newco by the manager's company and a second on the extraction of the gain from that company or on its liquidation. However, interest relief should be available to such a company, whether it is an investment or trading company, on what is known as a "charge on income". This will be true for any UK bank interest, but there will be no relief for "short" interest (for example, on an overdraft) paid to anyone else.

In connection with capital tax planning, part of a manager's investment may be made by a trust (generally of which he or she, or a member of his or her family, is the settlor). Unfortunately, a trust will not be able to obtain interest relief. Neither will relief be available to a person who borrows money to settle on a trust. A possible way out of this problem is for the manager to continue to hold the shares, but to grant an option to the trustees. If the manager is not the settlor, the grant of the option may make him or her an additional settlor for tax purposes.

Income tax treatment on shares

In a buy-out, managers will arguably acquire their shares by reason of their employment by, or directorships of, Target or "any other company". It would be unwise to rely on an argument that they acquire these shares as entrepreneurs.

Charges to income tax generally arise in two situations: on any amount by which the price at which management acquires shares falls short of the market value; and if a "chargeable event" occurs while they still own the shares.

A charge is generally unlikely to arise at the time of acquisition as, in any Newco structure, the price at which the buy-out takes place, and at which backers subscribe for shares, will normally be freely negotiated. There is, however, one trap which should be avoided. Backers may invest in more than one way (for example, ordinary shares and running yield redeemable preference shares). A backer may well assess the overall return in terms of the total investment. Thus, the price at which the backer subscribes for ordinary shares could conceivably be different (and higher) than the price at which management subscribes for ordinary shares. This situation invites a "market value" argument – and an immediate income-tax charge on the management.

Where there is a "chargeable event", and the company concerned is not a "dependent subsidiary" (more of which below), an income tax charge will arise on the increase in value that is attributable to that event.

Any of the following is a chargeable event:

– the removal or variation of a restriction to which the shares are subject;
– the creation, or variation of, a right attaching to the shares;
– the removal or variation of a right relating to other shares in the company; or
– the imposition of a restriction over other shares in the company, or the variation of a restriction to which such other shares are subject.

Certain events which would otherwise be chargeable events are excepted. Fortunately these, and the conditions attaching, need not be considered in detail, as in practice there is often a simple solution. This is to enshrine all rights and restrictions for all shares in the Memorandum and Articles before subscription. Even if the value subsequently increases as a result of the operation of the rights and restrictions, there is no removal or variation of them in terms of the chargeable events rules: the rights and restrictions remain as prescribed in the first place.

The classic share structure in a buy-out involves the management holding ordinary shares, and the backers (whatever else they hold) holding shares that represent a "slice" that is dependent on the results, or flotation, or sale price. These ratchet arrangements are best arranged on a declining basis – by means of provisions in the Memorandum and Articles as explained above – so that effectively they give the backer a fixed capital return on an element of his investment. True equity investment by the backers can then be by way of an appropriate holding of ordinary shares.

It is particularly important to ensure that Newco is not a "dependent subsidiary". Essentially, this is any subsidiary which does business with its parent or fellow subsidiaries, or where the value of its shares is increased by means of intra-group transactions. There is also a certification requirement, which is frequently overlooked. If shares are acquired in a company which is a dependent subsidiary at the outset, the whole growth in the value of the shares over the period of ownership is charged to income tax. It is unusual for shares to be held in a subsidiary as a result of a buy-out, as no one corporate shareholder normally holds the majority of the ordinary shares in Newco. If the company subsequently becomes a dependent subsidiary, only the increase in value attributable to the period of its dependency is charged to income tax.

The tax rules surrounding income tax charges and shares are extremely complex. In this area, perhaps more than any other, management will need adequate advice especially if certain members of the team are to take shares partly paid.

Income for management

The management's income will be limited under the deal that is struck with the backers. Tax and national insurance will apply in the ordinary way to income that is drawn as salary. Clearly, a baseline salary is sensible, but tax-efficient pension arrangements should not be overlooked. As a general rule, management should not rely entirely on a capital appreciation of their shares to provide for their retirement.

At the time of writing, it is possible that the upper-earnings limit on employee national insurance contributions may be removed. If it is, dividends (as compared to salary, and other national-insurance efficient ways of providing income) will become more attractive. The commercial structure of a buy-out needs to be carefully designed: it is difficult to switch from salary to dividends once the share structure has been set up. Benefits in kind, other than those relating to cars and most non-cash bonus schemes, do not presently attract National Insurance. If bonuses are to be paid to management, the possibility arises of payment in, for instance, strategic metals. These schemes may prove to be short-lived; at any rate, extremely careful drafting is required.

Capital gains and inheritance tax planning

This subject is worthy of a whole book to itself, involving as it does a consideration of the use of trusts. However, some broad pointers may prove useful.

If other family members are to benefit (typically children or grandchildren), then the best time to plan is at the time of the buy-out. It is difficult to avoid income tax if any trust is a parental settlement on minor children; however, if the income is accumulated, it will not be deemed to be that of the parent, and will therefore be taxed at 35 per cent. It is not generally possible to avoid capital gains tax, whether the settlement is UK resident or offshore, unless there is a non-domiciled settlor. However, an income in possession trust, under which the settlor and his or her spouse are excluded from benefit, has a tax-rate advantage, in that it suffers capital gains tax at a flat rate of 25 per cent (rather than the 40 per cent rate paid by those in the higher income-tax brackets).

With regard to inheritance tax, making an early transfer to a trust that may be tax-exempt can have significant advantages. In particular, there will then be no valuation difficulties on a cash settlement, and there are also no difficulties about whether any gain on a later gift or settlement of shares is eligible for a hold-over election in respect of the capital gain. All that is required with regard to the inheritance tax is for the settlor to survive the transfer of value for seven years, or to insure against early death in such a way as to provide cash to pay the tax.

There is really only one way for management to avoid capital gains tax – and that is emigration. This is obviously a rather drastic step, and anyway, a flotation or sale may well require the continued presence of the management for a period. A slightly less extreme alternative is for management to dispose of their shares at a time when they are not resident or ordinarily resident in the United Kingdom – although they must remain non-residents for at least three years. This will need planning, and a careful selection of country, there is little point in avoiding a UK capital gains tax bill only to pay an equivalent tax elsewhere.

There are also capital gains avoidance schemes that involve offshore companies; these are risky ventures and may not succeed at all.

Using a trust, it is possible to avoid capital gains tax altogether on an appointment of funds out of the trust to beneficiaries, if the exit route for the trustees is via a purchase of own shares by the company. This is more likely to be possible on a sale, as opposed to a flotation, and is a rather complex process. Subject to the degree of pre-ordination, it is also vulnerable to attack by the Inland Revenue under their so-called "new approach".

For inheritance tax purposes, a holding by one manager of over 25 per cent is likely to qualify for 100 per cent business property relief; a holding of less than 25 per cent will qualify for 50 per cent relief. Shareholdings qualify for relief provided they are owned for two or more years and are not fully listed. On death, the shares must be business property in the hands of the beneficiary for relief to be available.

Management should not consider capital tax planning solely in relation to their shares, but generally. Most buy-out team members will not have substantial wealth but, if the bought-out business is successful, they are likely to become very wealthy indeed.

Newco and Target

All but the smallest buy-outs generally proceed with a Newco, as the level of financing required is above that at which personal borrowings are a realistic proposition. On the assumption that what is to be acquired is a company rather than assets, Newco's and Target's tax affairs will be inextricably linked and are best considered together.

Asset purchase

Unless there are tax-adjusted trading losses in Target, from management's point of view a purchase of assets and undertaking will generally be the best action with regard to taxation. Such a purchase ensures a full tax basis in the assets acquired (rather than the historic basis in Target). What is best for the acquiror is generally not best for the vendor, whose interests usually hold sway in this area. Thus asset-purchase buy-outs are comparatively rare, and will not be considered further here. However, as a first step in formulating a buy-out proposal, the possibility of an asset purchase should be considered and evaluated.

Investment or trading company

For tax purposes, the Newco must be either an investment or trading company. If it is neither, there will be no relief for interest on any debt element of the finance for the buy-out.

If a single company is to be acquired, it may not be possible for the Newco to gain investment company status, as the definition of an investment company (for tax purposes) is one in which the business consists of the making and managing of investments, and in which the principal part of the income is derived therefrom. If Target is more than one company, or a group of companies, this potential problem diminishes. However, it is still necessary to meet the second part of the test. The dividend income from Target (under a group income election to avoid payment of advance corporation tax, if Newco itself is not paying dividends) is the answer. However, care is still needed as, typically, the management team will be remunerated by Newco and the cost plus a mark-up will be recovered from Target. Although it is arguable that, when applying the "income" test, what is to be compared is investment income and profit on management charges, some Inspectors have advanced the argument that the primary business of Newco is making management charges – not making and managing investments.

Relief for interest cost for Newco

Assuming that investment company status is established, the next question concerns how Newco may obtain tax relief for interest on its debt. Fortunately the interest is treated as an expense of management and can be group relieved against Target's profits. In order to put Newco's profit and loss account back to where it was before the interest was paid (at least in part), the group relief can be paid for by Target without tax effect at any price up to pound for pound for the losses surrendered. However, this raises the spectre of Target giving prohibited financial assistance for the purchase of its own shares and hence legal advice should be sought. Financial assistance may be permitted provided certain formal steps are taken. Investment companies may group relieve excess management expenses, or carry them forward, but they may not carry them back. If Target makes a tax-adjusted loss, any excess management expenses in Newco in the same year will become difficult to use. There is no simple way around this problem if it arises.

In order to resolve any problems concerning the status of Newco as an investment company, and to simplify the structure, Target is often rendered dormant by transferring its assets, undertaking and liabilities to Newco immediately after the acquisition. In appropriate cases, it may be possible to convert all or part of Newco's interest cost into what is known as a "trade charge". Interest of this kind can be used to augment a trading loss for carry forward, but not for carry back – unless it is interest paid to a UK bank, when it is treated as a trading expense and thus may be carried forward or back. This creates much more flexibility, but Newco's interest cost can never be carried back against Target's prior profits.

The technique is for Newco to borrow further monies to acquire Target's net assets, and for Target to dividend the money back, permitting Newco to repay its original borrowings. If market value is paid, arguably there is no prohibited financial assistance, as Newco pays cash, and a lawfully paid dividend is excepted from the definition of financial assistance. However, if Target's issued share capital is of any size, there will be a cash balance in Target which may only be lent to Newco if the formal steps for permitted financial assistance can be implemented. Clearly legal advice is required. On the transfer of assets to Newco, Newco will "step into the shoes" of Target for those tax purposes that relate to capital allowances and trading losses. If there are trading losses, it may be necessary for all liabilities to be taken on by Newco, as otherwise there will be a restriction on the amount of losses transferred.

The date when Target ceases to trade will count as the end of a tax period. If this is a date other than Target's normal accounting date, and Target is profitable, then there will obviously be an acceleration of the payment date for corporation tax purposes.

Assets passing from Target to Newco will do so within a capital gains group and there will be neither gain nor loss. Indexation relief effectively continues by reference to Target's base value.

There should be no stamp duty cost on the intra-group asset transfer, as there is an exemption available on a claim made by statutory declaration in these circumstances. Care will be needed if bank borrowings are being "switched" as envisaged, in order not to fall foul of anti-avoidance provisions.

Accounting for the transfer of Target's trade to Newco can pose a strain on the latter's profit and loss account. If the transfer is effected at market value, Newco is likely to have to pay for goodwill, which will either have to be written off or amortised in its own profit and loss account. A substantial dividend from Target will not help as, Target having been rendered dormant, the cost of investment in Target will have to be written down to net asset value. The alternative is to transfer goodwill for £1, provided that it is possible to take the appropriate formal steps to avoid prohibited financial assistance. No transfer of an undervalued asset should be made from Target to Newco, if Target's profit and loss account is in deficit, or will thereby be caused to go into deficit. Such a transfer will constitute an unlawful distribution and reduction of capital; this cannot be cured by taking the permitted route of financial assistance.

Tax clearance

Only one formal tax clearance is likely to be relevant to a buy-out, and that concerns anti-avoidance provisions relating to transactions in securities. Clearance may not be needed in all cases, but should be obtained if there is to be anything other than a normal dividend pre- or post-acquisition, or if there is to be a transfer of Target's trade to Newco. The need for clearance can arise in other circumstances and each case must be examined on its own merits.

VAT grouping

Unless the business operated by Target is exempt from VAT forming a VAT group between Newco and Target will generally be beneficial for input VAT recovery on those costs arising after the VAT group is formed.

Shares issues by Newco to subscribers in the EC will constitute an exempt supply and any associated VAT will be irrecoverable irrespective of the VAT grouping position. However, if shares are issued to subscribers both within and outside the EC, there will be scope for making partial or full recovery of any associated VAT.

Acquisition costs

On the assumption that Newco starts life as an investment company, its costs in considering making the acquisition of Target (until the date of the actual decision to invest) should be deductible as management expenses. Costs associated with raising loan finance should be deductible under specific provisions, provided that the detailed conditions are met.

If Newco is immediately turned into a trading company, the rather more generous case-law derived deduction for part of the acquisition costs as expenses of management is likely to be denied. This is because Newco does not qualify as an investment company – rather it is an intending trading company. Nevertheless, it acquires shares in the first instance, and thus cannot apportion acquisition costs to assets acquired on the subsequent transfer of Target's assets and trade.

Stamp duty

On an acquisition of shares of a company incorporated in Great Britain, stamp duty of a half per cent is effectively an unavoidable cost. If a stampable document is not presented for stamping within two months of the contract to acquire Target, a liability to stamp duty reserve tax arises instead.

Advance corporation tax

If Newco is financed partly on the basis that there will be a running yield on shares, it will be necessary to ensure that Newco and Target together will have sufficient capacity each year to absorb the advance corporation tax liability arising against mainstream corporation tax at the earliest opportunity. Prudence dictates that full advance corporation tax utilisation should be achievable on the minimum acceptable level of profit projections.

If there has been no hive up of assets and trade from Target to Newco, taxable profits will inevitably arise mainly in Target. Thus the dividends it pays should generally be "franked" (despite the group income election which will be made) in order to get the advance corporation tax in the right place in the first instance. This is especially true in view of the possibility of a three-year carry back for a trading loss, should Target unfortunately have a bad year in the future. A company can carry back advance corporation tax that it has paid itself (but not the advance corporation tax surrendered to it) for six years, although this will not be possible against pre-acquisition periods if there has been a major change in the nature or conduct of the company's trade. Thus it may be possible to offset previously used advance corporation tax, displaced by trading losses carried back, against the mainstream corporation tax of earlier years.

Pre-acquisition losses in Target

Losses in Target prior to acquisition by Newco may or may not be available to set against tax, depending on whether the vendor is a group which takes them by way of group relief, or their carry forward is denied as a result of the change of ownership rules. Whether or not Target's losses are surrendered to the vendor group is a commercial matter which needs to be sorted out at an early stage in buy-out negotiations.

The carry forward of trading losses is denied in the case of a change of ownership where there is a major alteration in the nature or conduct of the trade within three years of either side of the transaction. If Target has been loss making, some Inspectors seem to think that a move to profits must involve a major change in the nature or conduct of the trade. Commercial, not tax, considerations should determine the managers' strategy – but managers should be aware that significant amounts of tax may be involved.

Similar rules apply to the carry forward and carry back of advance corporation tax over a change of ownership.

For these reasons, when assessing price, trading losses and advance corporation tax carried forward in Target will normally be ignored; their use after the acquisition should be viewed as a bonus.

Capital allowances disclaimer

If Target has unrelieved tax-adjusted trading losses, a disclaimer of capital allowances should be considered. This, of course, presupposes that the vendor is not taking Target's losses by way of group relief.

A disclaimer of capital allowances will reduce the amount of losses that are vulnerable to a denial of carry forward over the change in ownership, and will produce higher tax depreciation in the form of capital allowances when Target is owned by Newco.

Target's tax affairs

Management, Newco and backers will be concerned that Target's tax affairs are up to date and in order. The taxes they will focus on include corporation tax, income tax, VAT, PAYE and stamp duty, plus any overseas taxes. Given that management will usually not have conducted Target's tax affairs, warranties and indemnities will be sought and usually given. However, these may not extend to PAYE and VAT, if these taxes have been administered by management.

The warranties and indemnities should be considered only as a final insurance. The reason is straightforward: Target will still have to pay any tax due if there is claim against the vendor that is disputed.

A comprehensive tax due diligence exercise should therefore be carried out on behalf of Newco. Any potential liabilities for tax, interest or penalties should be assessed, and specific obligations should be placed on the vendor. The vendor should also be made responsible for eliminating any arrears in the taxation affairs of Target.

The scope and extent of warranties and indemnities given by the vendor in the case of a buy-out are generally much less than in the case of a third-party sale. The issue should therefore be addressed early on in the discussions, but any agreement should be made subject to the findings of the due diligence work.

In the case of known potential liabilities, a retention of part of the purchase price by Newco (perhaps in a stakeholders' account) will protect Newco against a cash embarrassment if the liability crystallises.

Pre-sale dividends

If the vendor wishes to extract a pre-sale dividend, this will either be under a group income election or Target will have to pay advance corporation tax. In either case, the cash position of Target needs to be considered, and the timing effect of setting advance corporation tax against mainstream liability by Target needs to be assessed.

Care needs to be exercised if a pre-sale dividend is to be paid under group income election. At some stage in the sale process, the election will become invalid – and this point needs to be determined. If there is any risk of Target being required to pay advance corporation tax, appropriate protection should be obtained from the vendor in the share sale agreement.

Base value of Target's assets

Whether or not there is to be a realisation of surplus or redundant assets after the buy-out, Newco should insist that it obtains full details of the acquisition history of Target's assets as a matter of good housekeeping.

If there are likely to be asset realisations, an assessment should be made of any likely tax liabilities arising. The disposal of, for instance, a surplus property, may give rise to a capital gain or loss. The sale proceeds of surplus plant and equipment may or may not be covered by the "pool" of tax written-down value. Even if there is no immediate liability, the capital allowances available to Target will be reduced.

If there are surplus assets, the question arises as to whether any tax liability arising on their realisation should be borne by the vendor. From management's point of view, this is probably best dealt with by fixing the price offered. However, information to assess tax liabilities on asset realisations may not be available at the offer stage. An alternative approach is to insist on providing for deferred taxation in the completion accounts, having set an appropriate level of net assets that are required to be revealed. In practice, resolving the question of who is to bear tax on asset realisations can be a particularly difficult negotiating point. It is thus best raised early, and dealt with in Newco's offer.

Intra group asset transfers

Where a company leaves a group within six years of having had an asset transferred to it intra group, a disposal and re-acquisition at market value is deemed to have arisen. Any capital gain arising is taxable in the accounting period during which the company leaves the group.

Conventionally, it is accepted that the liability should fall on the vendor, but the rules trigger the gain in the Target – although this can, in most cases, be covered in whole or part by group relief surrendered by the vendor group for tax periods ending after 30 September 1993. From Target's perspective, it is unsatisfactory to rely on warranties and indemnities even with a cash retention, as it may not be possible to quantify the tax liability accurately – particularly as valuations need to be agreed with the Inland Revenue.

The safest course is to require the vendor to transfer the asset intra group before the buy-out, and for Newco or Target to acquire the asset contemporaneously with the buy-out. These steps may increase the stamp duty but, on the basis that the whole matter is a vendor problem, negotiations should proceed on the basis that the vendor picks up any additional costs.

Vendor

Pre-sale dividend

If the vendor faces a capital gain on the sale of shares in the buy-out, it will look to reduce or eliminate the gain. One way of achieving this (if the vendor is a company) is to extract a pre-sale dividend. As noted above, the issue of advance corporation tax needs to be considered. It will also be necessary to check that the dividend is not being paid out of an intra-group profit, as this will have no effect on the capital gains front. If the dividend is abnormal in amount (as defined in the transactions in securities anti-avoidance provisions), consideration should be given to obtaining a formal tax clearance.

If the vendors are individuals or are trusts, a pre-sale dividend, with advance corporation tax being paid by Target, will generally be beneficial; it will produce a lower overall tax bill, provided the vendor's base values, indexation relief, capital losses and any available retirement relief are covered by the "remaining" sale proceeds.

Where there is a trust shareholder in Target, consideration should be given to a purchase of own shares in such a way that it is not afforded capital gains treatment (that is, it gives rise to dividend treatment for tax purposes for Target). In appropriate cases, it may be possible to achieve a totally tax-free realisation for the trust and beneficiaries. As mentioned above, in the discussion about capital gains and inheritance tax, this is a complex transaction.

Capital losses

Vendors should ensure that any available capital losses may be set against a gain arising on the sale of Target. If the vendor is a member of a group, there may well be a "capital loss" company to which Target should be transferred before sale. It should be noted that the use of capital losses that have been "bought in" since 1987 has been rendered ineffective by the Finance Act 1993. However, the use of an existing (or purchase of a new) excess management expenses company, and the routing of the sale of Target through it, should still be considered.

Care is needed in two areas of a pre-sale intra-group transfer of Target. In order for stamp duty exemption to be available, certain kinds of arrangements involving third parties must not exist. A transfer before the "heads of terms" stage is reached is therefore advisable. The second point concerns beneficial ownership. Although the Inland Revenue accept an efficient use of capital losses within groups, Inspectors will raise a beneficial ownership objection in appropriate cases. There must, therefore, be no contract (written or oral) to sell Target before the intra group transfer has been effected.

Whether the vendor is a company or not, it will be sensible to ensure that any prospective disposal which will generate a capital loss occurs in the same tax period. For companies, this will usually be the accounting year, and for individuals and trusts it will be the year to 5 April.

Amounts due from Target to vendor

When Target is a member of a group, the situation often arises that the price at which a sale is to be made is for the shares and inter-company debt. If inter-company debt exceeds the prospective sale proceeds, the appropriate way to proceed is to assign £1 to the shares to be sold, and the balance of the proceeds to inter-company debt. This leaves some inter-company debt to be eliminated.

Waiver will probably be acceptable, provided the debt has not arisen as a result of management charges or other items which have given rise to a tax deduction for Target. In this case, waiver will give rise to a deemed trading receipt in Target. There is a concern that waiver may, in any event, give rise to a trading receipt to Target. It is therefore best to proceed by way of conversion into share capital. Whether or not, and the extent to which, the vendor thereby creates a capital gains base cost in the new shares, depends on the amount by which the market value of its investment increases as a result.

Tax warranties and indemnities

The vendor's position is, of course, the opposite to that taken by the management and Newco (as discussed earlier). Suffice to say, if the vendor has had responsibility for tax matters, the case for warranties and indemnities will usually be irresistible. However, the vendor should seek to limit its exposure both as to the period of time in which claims can be made, and the maximum monetary value.

The role of the lawyer

A management buy-out will involve a number of lawyers, each instructed to represent a specific interest: the vendor, the management team, or one or more financiers. It is the role of the lawyers to ensure that the documentation defines the relationships between numerous parties – all of whom are liable to have quite distinct requirements owing to their particular interests – and to ensure that the important issues are identified at an early stage in the transaction, so that they can be resolved in a timely manner. This chapter highlights some of these issues and explains how they might be resolved.

Initiating the buy-out

As soon as a management team begins to contemplate a buy-out, its members will need legal advice so that they can clarify the various duties that they owe.

Existing duties to employer

Before a management team approaches its employer, who will usually be the vendor, or a management team starts to formulate its plans, regard must be had to the duties its members owe to their employers. If the team's members are Directors of the target then they will owe fiduciary duties to their companies, quite apart from any contractual or common law duties that they owe as employees. A Director must at all times act in the best interests of his company, and he would be in breach of that duty if he were to try to organise a buy-out without the approval of his Board. Although an employee's duties to his employer are not as onerous as a Director's duties to his company, there will almost certainly be provisions in the employment or service agreements which will be relevant. For example:

– Is the individual required to spend his whole time and attention in furthering the company's interests?

– Are there restrictive covenants preventing him being employed in a competing business (particularly relevant in a buy-in)?
– If there are restrictions, are they limited to non-solicitation of customers and/or employees?

An instance of these issues arising in practice occurred when two particular individuals planned to leave one of the divisions of a public relations business – well known for the speed and aggression with which it went to court to prevent employees leaving and setting up on their own. After carefully analysing the various restrictive covenants that bound them, these individuals were able to resist completely the various efforts made to prevent them starting up on their own.

Approaching the vendor

Having established the legal duties of the individuals concerned, the next stage is the approach to the vendor. A buy-out team is not in any different position to an ordinary third party purchaser in terms of conflicts of interest. However, the buy-out team should always recognise that if the approach is unexpected it may well fundamentally alter the relationship between the management and the employer, a consequence the management team must recognise and address. (see Chapter Two for further discussion of this issue).

Even after the management team have broached the subject with the vendor, the problem of conflicting loyalties does not go away. Before the deal can complete there will probably be long, and sometimes difficult, negotiations with the vendor. It is quite possible that the transaction may fail some time after the management have had robust discussions with their employers. This may make it difficult for their previous relationship to continue. One way in which the lawyers can help protect against this problem is by assisting in, or even taking a leading role in the negotiations themselves. Particularly in the early stages, it is often helpful for the management to have their lawyer take up the difficult commercial points, as well as the legal ones, in the negotiations.

Confidentiality undertakings

Before the management team are able to disclose confidential information relating to the target company to third parties (including potential investors), both they and any recipients are likely to be required to sign confidentiality undertakings. These are becoming increasingly sophisticated and often include provisions which do not relate to confidentiality at all – restrictive covenants, arrangements on costs, and undertakings not to make a bid without board approval. Needless to say, these undertakings need to be carefully reviewed and not simply signed as presented.

Quoted companies

Buy-outs of quoted companies are quite rare, and although much of the above applies equally to quoted and unquoted companies, there are a number of special considerations for public companies. These include the need to recognise that management must approach independent Directors who have no ongoing interest in the buy-out and who themselves must take prompt independent advice. In addition, and most importantly, is the obligation (imposed by the Takeover Code) to ensure that all offerors or potential offerors are given, on request, equal access to information. Accordingly, information generated by the management of the target company, in their management capacity, which is passed to the financiers, will also have to be passed both to other potential offerors and to the independent Directors of the target.

Costs

Management must recognise that on most buy-outs they will need lawyers and possibly financial advisers, and that the equity house will insist on an accountant's long form report and that all these must be engaged/commissioned well before there is any certainty that the transaction will complete. There is therefore a risk that management will be left to pay some of the costs if the deal 'aborts'. There are a number of ways in which a management team can try to deal with this:

– They may be able to negotiate a contribution from the vendor to cover the costs of putting together an offer. This does happen, particularly where a vendor initiates a sale and wants to give the management a fair chance of buying the business in the face of competition from trade buyers. A further protection, where the deal is subject to the approval of the vendor's shareholders, is to provide that if that approval is not given, then the vendor is responsible for some or all of the purchaser's costs – most of which will have been incurred by the time contracts are exchanged.
– Where the target is a private company, it may be possible for the procedure under Section 155 of the Companies Act to be used to enable the target company itself to make a contribution to the buy-out team's costs[1]. The amount of that contribution will, under the Companies Act, reduce the distributable profits of the target company. This option is particularly helpful where a family-owned business is being acquired, and the family are reluctant to put their hands in their own pockets, but are willing to allow the company itself to make a contribution.
– The third source of funding is from the equity investor itself. Different equity houses have different policies on this, but it is not unusual for the risk of the acquisition costs and accountant's report to be borne by the equity investor, although the management would usually be expected to be responsible for dealing with the abort risk on the cost of their personal legal advice. .

---

[1]This procedure is contained in that part of the Companies Act which generally prohibits financial assistance being given by a company for the acquisition of its own shares. Many textbooks and articles explain this procedure in detail, and the mechanics are not dealt with in this chapter; however, the rules and procedures are referred to briefly in the section below entitled "Financial assistance".

Whatever the result of any discussions on costs, it is always wise to try to negotiate a 'lock-out' agreement whereby the vendor agrees that it will not negotiate with any third party for a period of time.

The acquisition

Most of the legal issues which arise on the acquisition aspect of a buy-out are common to any acquisition. The question as to whether or not shares or assets are to be acquired is no different in the case of a management buy-out, although on a share acquisition (as opposed to an assets acquisition) the financial assistance provisions under the Companies Act restrict the target company's ability to charge its assets to the banks. Other factors which will be taken into account are the extent to which liabilities are to be left behind, the need for commercial trading agreements to be assigned or novated, the need for new regulatory licences, and tax considerations relating principally to the ability to preserve tax losses or, importantly from a vendor's point of view, whether any tax charge will lie on a sale of assets as opposed to shares.

Three of the particular issues which arise on buy-outs are:

– the effect of the purchaser's limited cash resources;
– the negotiation on the warranties; and
– the ability of the new group to stand alone and independent from its parent.

Cash

It is often the case that on a buy-out the purchase price will be linked directly to the value of the assets acquired, as shown in completion accounts to be drawn up by the parties following completion. An amount equal to an estimate of the net assets will be paid at completion and there will then be a pound for pound adjustment to the purchase price once the final net assets acquired have been determined.

The difficulty that arises for a buy-out vehicle with fixed cash resources is that it cannot enter into an open-ended commitment to pay further cash to a vendor. Notwithstanding that the fixed assets may have increased, or there may have been an unexpected increase in working capital, so that the purchaser has acquired more assets, it simply does not have the liquidity to pay for the increase. Vendors will be reluctant to cap the price because to do so would run the risk that they would not receive value for the assets being sold. The problem can be dealt with in a number of ways:

– The purchaser and its accountants, through their due diligence exercise, can satisfy themselves as to the amount and mix of assets to be acquired. The purchaser can then ensure that there is sufficient headroom in its financing to allow for a suitable margin of error in the determination of the value of the assets at completion.
– Provisions can be included in the Acquisition Agreement deferring any further consideration that may be payable once the net asset figure has been determined, to the extent that the assets acquired are not liquid. Clearly, if net

assets have increased because of a build-up of cash, there will be no difficulty in the purchaser making the further payment. If, however, the net assets have increased because a new piece of equipment has been purchased out of the target's cash resources then either the purchaser needs time to find the additional finance or it needs to be made clear to the vendor that it must control the net asset position of the target business so that a cap on the purchase price can be agreed.
– Where the net assets have increased because of a temporary increase in working capital, it should be sufficient to negotiate a delay before any additional consideration has to be paid, so that the working capital can unwind. Thus, if net assets are higher because stock and debtors are higher than expected then, depending on the nature of the business, a reasonable delay between completion and payment should be negotiated to allow the debtors to be paid and the cash generated to enable the purchaser to pay the further consideration.
– Where the purchaser is buying assets and not shares, the simplest solution is to provide that if the completion accounts show that the purchaser has acquired more assets than it can afford, it simply returns some of those assets (e.g. debtors) to the vendor.

Generally, the difficulty can be resolved satisfactorily, although it should be noted that this is not a matter that can be adequately dealt with by warranty. Even if a vendor were prepared to warrant that net assets would not exceed a given figure, it would be difficult for a purchaser to show the loss it had suffered by acquiring more assets than it expected; much more importantly, by the time the matter came to court the purchaser would have long since run out of cash.

A similar problem arises where the completion accounts show that the purchaser is acquiring the amount of net assets that it was expecting, but that the mix of those assets is unexpected. For example, prior to completion, the vendor may have vigorously collected in debtors and left creditors unpaid for longer than normal. If the additional cash that would thereby arise in the business is used to repay borrowings or buy more stock or fixed assets, then the new owners will be faced with a cash crisis immediately following completion. This problem should be more theoretical than practical if the management team can control the cash position. However, the only effective legal comfort that can be obtained is a covenant in the Acquisition Agreement by the vendor that, to the extent that the mix of assets is unexpected, it will provide additional cash to the business.

Warranties
This is an area which poses particular problems in a buy-out. On the basis that the vendor is receiving a proper price for the target, it should be prepared to give the normal commercial and taxation warranties and indemnities which any buyer would seek. In practice, however, the vendor may be extremely reluctant to give full warranties and indemnities if the target company has been managed autonomously by the buy-out team, with the vendor's responsibility and knowledge extending at most to the central finance and taxation function.

As a consequence of the vendor's reluctance to give warranties, they may be requested from management in favour of the equity investors in the Subscription and Shareholders Agreement. However, in purely financial terms, warranties and indemnities from the management team regarding the status of the target are normally worth only a fraction of the cash subscribed by the equity investors. Therefore, those investors will normally insist on fairly comprehensive warranties from the vendor in the same way as an independent trade purchaser.

The next difficulty is that the vendor will often throw the warranties back to the management team on the basis that they are the people who have been running the business. This may be done on the basis of the vendor asking for a non-legally binding comfort letter from the management to the effect that the vendor can give warranties without liability. In addition there are sometimes "gold under the floorboards" clauses whereby the vendor seeks to establish that the management is not hiding anything which would give the target company an immediate boost to earnings or cash following the completion of the buy-out. Even if warranties or comfort to this effect are not expressly sought from the management, the management (and consequently the equity investors) may find themselves in trouble if they hide any advantageous factors from the vendor. This would give rise to the risk of civil action for breach of duties owed to the management's employer, or even criminal action relating to dishonest concealment of material facts in connection with the sale of shares.

At the end of the day, a negotiated compromise will need to be achieved. This may be on the basis that the warranties which the vendor gives in relation to day-to-day trading matters (if given at all) are qualified by reference to its knowledge, or the vendor may retain a defence against claims for breach of warranty to the extent that the management knew, or even ought to have known, of the matters giving rise to the breach. The financiers will, however, usually insist on absolute warranties on the last audited accounts, title to the shares and constitutional matters, a full tax indemnity and, to the extent that they have been managed by the vendor centrally, warranties on pensions, property and insurance. In addition, the purchaser may seek a waiver from the vendor against any claims the vendor may have against the management team. This is because if there is a breach of warranty, the purchaser does not want to be in the position whereby any claim it makes against the vendor will simply result in a claim by the vendor against the management team running the newly acquired business. This is clearly a difficult area, and will often not be agreed by a vendor for the reasons mentioned above.

Independence

The third area which often requires attention and legal documentation on a management buy-out is the transitional arrangements in respect of those matters which have been managed centrally by a vendor. For example; tax, property, pensions and insurance arrangements covering the period whilst the new group is making its own independent arrangements. There will often be a transitional services agreement between the purchaser and the vendor to ensure that the administration of the new group can continue smoothly following completion.

It may also be the case that there has been significant trading between the target business and the vendor group. Whilst there may not have been any need for a formal agreement between parent and subsidiary, following completion the financiers will almost certainly insist on an "arms length" trading agreement between the new company and the vendor. Whilst the commercial terms of this agreement can be negotiated in the normal way by the management team, if a minimum level of trading is essential to support the financing structure then the financiers will need to be satisfied as to the pricing arrangements, length of the agreement and termination provisions. An important point to note is that the banks are unlikely to accept a provision (which might otherwise be normal) which gives the vendor the right to terminate the trading agreement in the event that the new group is put into receivership; if there is value in the trading agreement then the banks will want to take "security" over it, and there is no benefit to them if by appointing a receiver the trading arrangements cease. This is a sensitive matter which needs to be carefully explained to a vendor, because it is not an issue on which the banks are likely to be able to be flexible.

An example of where sophisticated agreements had to be entered into to ensure the new group's independence was the 1991 Brunner Mond buy-in, ICI's Soda Ash business in Cheshire. The business shared a site with ICI and, given the nature of the business, some of the most important documents related to the sharing of facilities and power, and included detailed provisions relating to the rights of one party to lay power lines and piping across the other's land.

The equity investment

Documentation

The principal documentation surrounding the company formed to act as the buy-out vehicle, generally referred to as "Newco", will be:

- The Subscription Agreement,
- The Articles of Association of the new company and
- The management Service Contracts.

The institutional lawyers will generally be responsible for preparing the initial drafts, but the management and their lawyers will need to understand the capital structure of the new company and negotiate and agree the terms of these documents. Although, no doubt, there will be tough and difficult negotiations between the management and the investors, it is important at the outset to understand the nature of the relationship: it shall be one of partnership, and therefore fundamentally different to the relationship between the Newco purchaser and the vendor as well as that between Newco and its bankers.

Share capital

There are usually three separate types of share capital, although these can be sub-divided into further classes.

The management's interest will usually take the form of ordinary share capital which will carry votes and will rank behind preference or preferred share capital as to dividend and return of capital. It may also be specifically prohibited from receiving dividends for a number of years. Management, in any event, will often prefer to receive income in other ways and leave as much cash in the business as possible – particularly if they have been offered the incentive of a growing proportion of the equity after a given period if the business performs beyond initial expectations. It should be remembered that equity investors will certainly wish to see the management team make a substantial commitment in cash terms, in order to reduce the likelihood of their walking away from the business. This will usually involve borrowing by the management team on which they will wish to try and obtain tax relief for interest payable.

In most relatively sophisticated structures, the investor is likely to require two types of share capital. First, Preference Shares ranking ahead of all other shares, which are entitled to a fixed cumulative preferential dividend and a right of redemption (at the subscription price) so that the investor receives repayment of part of its investment at a stated date or over a fixed period of time. In addition, it will require some preferred equity (Preferred Ordinary Shares or "A" Ordinary Shares) which will carry a dividend calculated on profit participation and rank ahead of the management's Ordinary Shares for all purposes. Thus, on any winding up or sale it would be the Preferred Ordinary Shares held by the investors which will be paid out before the Ordinary Shares, although the management should be able to negotiate a right to "catch up" with the institutions per share return, after which the institutions and management would rank equally. In addition, the Preferred Ordinary Shares rights might contain an incentive to the management to achieve an exit over a fixed period of time by providing that the dividend on the Preferred Ordinary Shares increases dramatically after the projected exit date has passed. It is also usual to include provisions for "interest" to become payable if dividends to institutions fall into arrears. Although called "interest", this additional payment is still a distribution for company law purposes, and is therefore treated as a dividend. Other value-enhancing rights that institutions try to negotiate include a right to receive a minimum sum on a sale (as well as a winding-up) and other default-type provisions that are normally found in debt arrangements rather than equity investments.

A further element of the equity-type funding might be some kind of subordinated debt or soft loan from the investor. This would have many of the characteristics of the Preference Shares, except that it appears on the balance sheet as a liability and ranks ahead of the preference share capital and equally with trade creditors. This type of loan stock is quite different from any senior or mezzanine debt that might be made available.

An interesting example of yet another type of equity funding was the buy-out of Rank Motorway Services. In that transaction, the banks were only prepared to lend if the equity investors gave legally binding commitments to fund a minimum level of capital expenditure in the business in certain circumstances. As well as subscribing for share capital, therefore, the investors assumed a contingent funding commitment.

Ratchets

Ratchets are arrangements under which management's share of the equity varies in accordance with the performance of the business. The number of types of ratchet, and their mechanics, is limited only by the financiers' imagination. However, they will generally operate by reference to the return on the institution's investment known as the internal rate of return (IRR). The equity investor will typically be looking for an IRR of around 30 – 35 per cent each year, depending on the maturity of the business; although it is worth trying to negotiate, it should not be assumed that management will automatically get the excess. The logic of the risk:reward ratio, from the investor's point of view, is not that simple.

The ratchet usually manifests itself in the form either of cumulative profit targets, or market capitalisation targets on a sale or listing, although one sometimes sees the higher maths required to calculate the actual IRR set out in the specific conversion or redemption rights of the ratchet shares. If the concept of a ratchet is agreed, and the first offer relates to cumulative profits only, management may be able to negotiate a market capitalisation ratchet. The argument is that even if management miss the profit ratchet, if the business is subsequently sold at a price which gives the institutions their required IRR, then management should not be penalised.

Transfers of shares by management

A thorny point which constantly arises on structuring the new company is the management's right to retain their shares if they leave, for whatever reason. Both the investors and the management team have a common interest: each member of the management team should consider what his view might be if one of his colleagues were dismissed in justifiable circumstances, or walked out to go to a competitor. Other shareholders may not be prepared to see that manager walk off with a potentially valuable shareholding and may therefore insist that his shares be transferred at a discount to their full value. Furthermore, he may well be replaced, and the shareholders will wish to ensure that any equity participation granted to the replacement does not entail dilution by the issue of new shares.

A tax problem may arise in this situation if the departing executive's shares are acquired by a new or existing member of management at an undervalue. A solution to this can be found in an approved share option scheme designed to benefit additional members of the management and employees, and in an employee share scheme under the Companies Act which can be funded by the company to buy and "warehouse" shares owned by those who are required to sell at a reduced price on leaving. Employee participation is discussed in more detail later on in this chapter. It is fair to say that where a manager dies or retires through ill health, there is sympathy for the view that not all of his shares should be required to be offered up for sale under compulsory transfer provisions.

Inevitably, there are quite a number of different circumstances which could arise which would justify the departing individual either being required to sell all of the shares owned without question; or being required to sell some of them at one price, some of them at another price; or being allowed to keep some of the shares. Whilst there is no easy answer to the problem, it is easier to be objective about these issues at the outset, and to set down firm rules, rather than having to deal with the problems as they arise: emotional considerations are always liable to outweigh the desire to make the correct business decision.

Warranties

Vendor and investors

As has been described in the context of the acquisition, the whole question of warranties on a management buy-out poses particular problems. As far as the equity investment is concerned, and the comfort that the equity investors are seeking, the first approach must be to negotiate the best possible warranties from the vendor before discussing management warranties.

Reality of management warranties

Regardless of the warranties regarding the target which are obtained from the Vendor, the equity investors will require the management to give warranties regarding their business plan, broadly that it has been properly and honestly prepared on the basis of reasonable assumptions.

Assuming that the management do have to give some warranties regarding the target, it is fair to say that equity investors will usually recognise that management is unlikely to be able to compensate them for their lost investment in the event of a breach of warranty. The purpose of these warranties is to focus the managers' minds and to ensure that they make a proper disclosure of information to the equity investors.

The management is not required to "underwrite" the accuracy of the information given to the equity investors, and therefore it is perfectly logical for the management to argue that all the factual warranties that they give should be to the best of their knowledge – having made reasonable enquiries. Even that concept may have to be qualified in that it may not be possible, for practical reasons, for management to make enquiries of all employees, customers and suppliers. If that principle can be agreed, then an honest and conscientious management team should derive substantial comfort. The reality is that the equity investor is unlikely, except in the worst of cases, to sue the individuals who are managing the business that it has invested in.

Class consents

Institutions

Management must be prepared for institutional backers to require that they be consulted, or their approval be given, not only for what might be called constitutional matters, but also for significant management matters as well. These types of control (which will be contained in the Articles and Shareholders Agreement) will operate either through a requirement that the institution's Board representative give his consent to various matters, or that the consent of the institutional shareholders themselves is required. In the case of larger, syndicated transactions the distinction is important, as it may not always be easy to obtain the class consent of the institutional investors quickly. It is therefore well worth spending the time deciding which matters are so fundamental that they should go back to the institutional shareholders, and which matters ought to be capable of approval by the institutions Board representative. Depending on the experience of the management team and the investor's house style, the level of hands-on involvement of the lead investor will vary. With common sense, this is an area which ought to be agreed relatively quickly and painlessly, but it can sometimes give rise to lengthy debate.

Management

More importantly, from the management's point of view, particularly where they do not have voting control of the new company, is the question of the class consents that management need to protect their investment. This is a difficult area, particularly when the investor tries to protect its position should the new company not prosper. In those circumstances, the institutions will not want to have to obtain the consent of the management team in order to carry out remedial action. On the other hand, the management team have struck a deal with the investors and, particularly if there is a ratchet, they will not want to be in a position in which they might easily be forced to abandon that deal. The debate will focus on the meaning of "failure" – although often the reality is that failure occurs when the banks say it has occurred.

Personal arrangements

Opportunity for tax planning

At the time of a buy-out, management ought also to consider their personal tax affairs. If all goes well, they should stand to make a substantial capital gain, and it is better to plan for that at this stage, rather than at the time the gain is realised. Notwithstanding the restrictions placed on the use of off-shore trusts by the Finance Act 1991, there is still scope for substantial tax planning.

Service Contracts

Service Contracts are primarily of protection to the individuals, rather than the company, in that they create a liability on the company in the event that it wishes to terminate the Service Contract. Whilst the restrictive covenants which are likely to be included are for the benefit of the company, these tend to be included in the Shareholders Agreement anyway. Whilst an individual might want a longer Service Agreement, this may be resisted by his colleagues or the investor. There is little point in the management team insisting on long-term contracts for themselves, if they will have to be re-negotiated by the company before a listing can be achieved.

Loan arrangements

In a large deal, the documents involved on the banking side might include a Senior Loan Agreement, a Mezzanine Loan Agreement, an Inter-Creditor Agreement (recording the relationship between the Senior and Mezzanine Debt) and the Security Documents which will be entered into by Newco and all members of the

Target Group in order to secure both Senior and Mezzanine Facilities.

One of the more obvious features about the debt side of a buy-out is the sheer bulk of documentation involved. The buy-in of BP's consumer-products division was a good example – the Main Facilities Agreement for the £128 million of senior loan underwritten by Bank of Scotland and others ran to 129 pages. In addition, there was a Mezzanine Agreement of similar proportion, together with a full cross Guarantee and Debenture structure for the Target Group, plus security documentation and funding arrangements in three other jurisdictions.

It is important to focus on the loan documents, since the covenants contained in them do, amongst other things, set out the rules by which the business will have to be run for the life of the loans. Individuals from the equity house and management team who are to look after the banking side should be identified at an early stage. Ideally, there should be a preliminary meeting between them and the lawyers to discuss the future plans for the business in some detail, so that sufficient flexibility can be built into the loan covenants to accommodate those plans so far as possible. A good example of how flexibility can be achieved was in the management buy-out of the lawnmower manufacturers, Atco-Qualcast. In that case, because the business was seasonal and could be affected by adverse weather conditions, a special "drought" provision was included in the Loan Agreement which, in certain circumstances, enabled the borrower to amend its repayment obligations.

The structure of Loan Agreements

It is essential to identify the main components contained in Loan Documents, because unless the importance of each component is understood it is difficult to understand the document as a whole and to negotiate it effectively.

Conditions precedent

This section of the Loan Agreement will list all those items which must be satisfied before the banks become obliged to lend the funds. These conditions become critical in those buy-outs where there is a gap between exchanging contracts and actually completing the deal. Apart from those conditions which are completely within the control of Newco and the management team, all other conditions to drawdown must also be conditions to the completion of the Acquisition Agreement. Otherwise, the Acquisition Agreement becomes unconditional but the banks are not obliged to provide the funds to Newco to enable it to pay the purchase price.

Margin protection

The next clause of commercial significance ensures that the bank's margin is protected. The cost to Newco of borrowing the funds is made up of three elements:

– Libor;
– the margin; and
– the associated costs.

Libor represents the cost to the banks of themselves borrowing the funds in the Inter-bank Market. Associated costs are the known costs to them of complying with the Bank of England special deposit requirements. The margin is therefore the element of profit which they have on the deal. As a result, the margin protection provisions in the Loan Agreement are designed to ensure that, no matter what happens, the banks will always receive that element of profit out of the deal.

Representations and warranties

It is important to understand the different function which warranties perform in a Loan Agreement, as compared to their function in an Acquisition Agreement. Essentially, when a vendor gives a warranty it makes a contractual promise that a certain state of affairs prevails in relation to the business being sold; if that proves to be incorrect then the purchaser can sue for the damages suffered.

In a Loan Agreement – on the other hand – the banks are not looking to the warranties to give them a right to sue the borrower. The purpose of the representations and warranties is to paint a picture of the financial soundness of the borrower, as of the date on which the loans are advanced. The representations and warranties are then repeated at regular intervals throughout the duration of the loan; if those representations can no longer be given it means that the financial soundness of the borrower is no longer assured, and the banks are entitled to call for the return of their money.

General Undertakings

The general undertakings section of the Loan Agreement is the section in which it is important to involve management (so far as it is possible) in the negotiations; this is because, in essence, the general undertakings will set out a list of "do's" and "don'ts" for the duration of the loans. For example, they may well prohibit the borrower from having any other borrowings other than those negotiated as part of the buy-out, entering into finance leases and from disposing of assets other than in the ordinary course. It is therefore important to consider the business plan and to try and build into the Loan Agreement the flexibility that the management need to run the business effectively and efficiently over the period of the loans.

Financial covenants

If there is one aspect of the Loan Document on which people should focus at an early stage, it is the financial covenants. Although it may be unfair to say so, the lawyers' experience is that not infrequently the equity house will have their own financial model demonstrating the anticipated performance of the business, the banks will have their model, and the management may have yet another model. The sooner that the participants in the transaction get together and agree the models, then the less likely it is that there will be a hold-up later on as everyone tries to match the projected performance to the financial covenants being set by the banks.

Events of default

These provisions speak for themselves. If any Event of Default occurs, then the banks are entitled to require their money back. In a buy-out situation, however, simply demanding the money back is actually not going to get the banks very far. What it usually means, in practice, is that if a default occurs the banks are entitled to review the basis upon which they are lending; they may require higher rates of interest to reflect the increased risks that they are running, given that the financial health of the company has deteriorated. At worst, it means that they can put in their own receiver and effectively take over the management of the business.

Inter-Creditor Agreement

The senior lenders will have the right to be paid-off before any other category of investor in the buy-out vehicle. Next in line is the mezzanine lender. The mezzanine loan will, by and large, reflect the same terms as the senior loan, but will only have the benefit of a second charge over the assets of the buy-out group. However, it will also be the case that the mezzanine loan will be subordinated to the interests of the senior lenders. It is worth emphasising the distinction between being a lender holding a second charge, and being a lender whose debt is subordinated to another debt. The holder of a second charge is, on a default by the borrower, entitled to step in, enforce its security and, subject to handing over enough of the proceeds to the senior lender as are necessary to repay the senior loan, use whatever is left to pay off its own debt. A subordinated lender, however, does not have this option. Unless the senior lender wants its debt to come in, the subordinated lender must sit and wait for its money.

Subordination has nothing to do with security, but is merely an agreement between the senior and junior lender. In a buy-out, this agreement manifests itself in the Inter-Creditor Agreement. The Inter-Creditor Agreement does two main things. First, it regulates the priority as between chargeholders; that is, it records that the senior lender has the first charge and the mezzanine lender has the second charge, and will set out the extent of the priority – the amount of money for which the senior lender ranks ahead of the mezzanine lender. The second thing that the Inter-Creditor Agreement does is to set out the contractual subordination – that is, the fact that the mezzanine lender cannot take steps to ask for its money back unless certain conditions are satisfied. Those conditions will invariably require that a default has occurred under the Mezzanine Loan Agreement, and that a period of time has elapsed after that default has occurred. This is the so-called "standstill period". The mezzanine lender must sit and wait for that period to expire before it can demand its money back, or enforce its security. This is always a crucial part of the negotiation. It is important for the question of standstill periods to be addressed, and for the Inter-Creditor Agreement to be looked at as soon as possible, because some of the most complicated arguments can arise over this document. The sooner these major elements can be dealt with, the more smoothly the transaction will proceed.

One other point on the Inter-Creditor Agreement which can be important to Newco is to provide for the possibility of the senior facilities being increased. If the senior facilities are (say) £20 million, then normally the Inter-Creditor

Agreement will provide that the priority of the senior banks is limited to £20 million. However, if Newco does hit trading difficulties and needs some further borrowings to tide it over a temporary period of difficulty, then it is obviously to its advantage only to have to negotiate with the senior lenders. If it can, therefore, be provided that increased facilities of a further (say) £2 million can be agreed without reference to the mezzanine lenders, this may prove useful in the future.

Financial assistance

It is impossible to have any discussion about the debt side of a buy-out without talking about financial assistance. As is well known, the target group of companies may only enter into Guarantees and Debentures to secure the acquisition debt incurred by Newco if the relevant provisions of the Companies Act are followed. Briefly, the directors of each target must make a statutory declaration to the effect that they have formed the opinion that for the period of one year following the date on which they given the Guarantees and Debentures, their particular company will be able to pay its debts as they fall due. This declaration is supported by an auditors' report. The process therefore involves all the directors of all subsidiary companies of the Target, who may or may not be involved in the buy-out process; if there is a lot of secrecy surrounding the transaction, the directors of subsidiaries may only learn of the buy-out at a very late stage. Given that there are criminal penalties if a statutory declaration is given without reasonable grounds, and given that in order properly to form a view about what their company's financial position will be after the buy-out they will need to see cash-flow figures for the whole buy-out group, this is an area which requires careful planning. It is not appropriate simply to summon all these directors to a completion meeting and ask them to give the statutory declarations.

Not only does the giving of statutory declarations need to be handled with sensitivity; it also raises the subject of the timing of the granting of the security. Where there are directors of target group subsidiaries who are not able to be brought into the confidential discussions and made aware of the buy-out proposals, then it is worth seeking the Bank's permission at an early stage that those subsidiaries do not give the Guarantees and Debentures until a reasonable period has elapsed after completion. This then provides time to explain the financial assistance procedure to the directors; to explain the factors they have to take into account, and to provide them with appropriate comfort that they can give their statutory declarations. A good example of this approach in practice was the management buy-out in 1989 of the Maxwell commercial printing interests by BPC Ltd. In that transaction, some 200 Directors at all levels within the group had to sign statutory declarations and the banks agreed that some declarations would be given at completion, some within two weeks and some within four weeks. A hall in the Barbican Centre was used to explain the process to the Directors; completion itself was quite an affair, as all those Directors had to be present to hold various Board Meetings. Whether the banks would be prepared to wait for their security in the current climate is another matter.

Vendor loans

It is increasingly common that, when the management team or equity investor have been unable to reach agreement with the vendor on price, the gap is bridged by some kind of vendor loan. This can vary from a simple obligation to pay a fixed sum in two or three years time, to arrangements in which the amount payable is dependent on the performance of the acquired business. One of the most complicated vendor loans arose in the buy-out of Anglian Windows from BET in December 1990. In that transaction, if the acquired business did not perform according to expectation, then both interest and principal could be converted into Deferred Shares. If, however, performance subsequently picked up, then those Deferred Shares could obtain value and there were further complex provisions converting the loan into Preference shares in the event of insolvency. There were many hours of detailed negotiation on the terms of this loan because it affected the acquisition, the debt arrangements and the share structure, and thus also affected all of the documentation on the most important aspects of the transaction. The lawyers involved were relieved that Anglian was successfully floated in 1992 and the vendor loan repaid without recourse to its detailed provisions.

The danger with these types of loan is that they can have an undue influence on the negotiations. A vendor loan will generally be introduced to support a level of debt which, according to normal commercial principles, the deal will not stand. The loan will represent the most junior creditor, but every covenant that is included in favour of the vendor represents a right of veto if the company does need to seek a waiver or modification of the provisions laid down at the time of the buy-out. When dealing with vendor loans, the clearer it can be made at the beginning of the negotiations that the loan is going to be a truly subordinated instrument – with very limited power to dictate what happens to the buy-out vehicle in the future – the less likely it will be that serious problems will arise, and significant concessions have to be granted, when actually negotiating its detailed terms.

Employee involvement

Introduction

Most buy-outs involve an employee share scheme of one sort or another. A selective share option scheme for management can be used as a form of ratchet. In addition, there may be reasons for extending the equity (or opportunities to acquire equity) to a larger proportion of the workforce.

A share scheme may act as an incentive and as a device to retain employees. Furthermore, some form of actual or potential equity participation may be an essential part of the overall package that is required to attract, motivate and retain a newcomer to the management team later on. If no equity has been reserved for this purpose, it may be necessary to enter into special bonus arrangements.

How to extend the equity

Options
From a mechanical point of view, there are various ways by which an individual

may acquire shares; the particular method concerned may involve differing tax consequences.

A particularly flexible method of providing rights to take-up shares is to grant options. The grant of an option would not normally involve the employee in any immediate outlay, but provides him with a certainty of his rights. The terms of options can easily incorporate performance conditions and targets, so that the option may only be exercised in certain specific circumstances and may be withdrawn from those who leave the Company. An option scheme is very flexible, and relatively cheap to establish and to operate.

The principal disadvantage of an option is that it does not involve the recipient in any commitment; the recipient is under no obligation to exercise the option, and so if the shares are not worth buying the recipient need never do so. Also, an option holder may not feel the same degree of involvement as a shareholder in the company.

Share issues

If commitment is required, then the employee could be offered the opportunity to acquire shares at the outset. This will provide an immediate identity of interest with the company, and the company's Articles can still provide for a clawback in the event of the employee leaving service. However, a direct employee share offer may involve the company and its management in a time-consuming exercise in order to provide employees with appropriate details of the company's share capital, and its financial information.

Methods of equity participation

Approved acquisitions

An approved acquisition is one that takes place under one of the three forms of Inland Revenue approved share scheme: the approved share option scheme (more commonly referred to as an Executive Share Option Scheme), the savings-related share option scheme, and the approved profit-sharing scheme. The first two, as the names suggest, provide rights to acquire shares in the form of options. In order to qualify for approval, the rules of the option scheme must incorporate various statutory limits on individual participation and, of particular importance in the context of a buy-out, the class of the company's share capital to be used must comply with a number of statutory requirements.

Under a profit-sharing scheme, the individual participants become the beneficial owners of shares allocated to them at the outset and for no payment. The shares will be registered in the name of a trustee for at least two years, and must remain so for a full five years if income-tax relief is to be obtained. Throughout that period, however, the participants will enjoy the full fruits of share ownership, save that they will not be able to vote the shares on a show of hands at a general meeting. Some profit-sharing schemes work on a matching basis, under which the employee has to buy some shares and voluntarily submit those shares to contractual restrictions in order to qualify for an appropriation of shares under the profit-sharing scheme. This obtains an immediate commitment from employees, yet provides them with shares at a discount of at least 50 per cent to their market value.

Share capital requirements under approved schemes

To prevent any manipulation of share value, only non-redeemable ordinary shares qualify for use under an approved scheme. If there is more than one class of ordinary share capital, either the majority of those shares in issue must be held otherwise than by directors and employees or other group companies, or the employees must control the company by virtue of their holdings of shares of that class.

Another difficulty for the buy-out company is that the legislation only allows a rather limited form of clawback of shares from former employees. As an exception to the general rule that restrictions must apply, if at all, to all shares of the same class, any clawback must operate against all directors and employees in respect of all their shares, howsoever and whensoever acquired.

Unapproved acquisitions

It may, as a result of the technical statutory requirements, be necessary or desirable to proceed with an unapproved arrangement. By definition, an unapproved arrangement does not enjoy the various forms of income-tax relief associated with approved schemes. As a result, the very acquisition of shares, the conferring of a right in respect of shares, the grant of an option and its exercise are each capable of giving rise to a charge to income tax as soon as the event occurs, whether or not the individual has received or can obtain out of the benefit conferred any cash whatsoever.

Unapproved schemes take a variety of forms and may be tailored more closely to individual requirements than approved schemes. If the taxable acquisition of shares occurs at the moment of "exit" from the buy-out, whether on a trade sale or a flotation, then the use of an unapproved scheme is not necessarily disadvantageous as compared with an approved scheme. With rates of income tax and capital gains tax equalised, it is quite likely that the total tax payable by virtue of the acquisition and immediate disposal of shares will be broadly the same whether the acquisition is approved or unapproved.

Employer share ownership plans

Frequently, one or more forms of share scheme are combined with an employee trust to form an employee share-ownership plan (ESOP). Almost invariably, the employee trust adopted is a discretionary trust with a class of beneficiaries that consists of the employees and former employees and their dependants of a particular company and its subsidiaries. Very few ESOPs are based on the statutory form of employee share-ownership trust (or ESOT), introduced by the Finance Act 1989, which imposes a number of rather unattractive conditions. Subsequent Finance Acts have introduced features in an attempt to make ESOTs more useful but it remains impossible to use an ESOT as a source of shares under a share option scheme, which is a substantial drawback.

A simple ESOP structure is shown in Exhibit 1. In the diagram, C is a management buy-out vehicle. At the time of the buy-out the ESOP trustee, T, borrowed funds from a bank and used them to acquire a substantial stake in C. At the same time C established an approved profit sharing scheme, APSS. Over a period of years since the buy-out, C has made contributions to T to service the interest on the loan. C has also made outright contributions to the APSS. These have been used by the APSS to buy shares from T for appropriation to employee participants in the APSS. The proceeds of sale of the shares has provided T with the funds with which to repay its principal debt to the bank.

There is, of course, only one real source of funding for an ESOP, namely the establishing company. Even where borrowings are from a third party at a commercial rate of interest, the Company will have to contribute to the trust in one way or another to service the debt. Almost invariably, it will also have to provide a guarantee. The Company could lend money directly to the ESOP, in which case it may be more efficient from a tax point of view to lend the funds interest free, and for the trustee of the ESOP to be obliged to waive dividends on any shares held. Extra care is required when, as will frequently be the case, the buy-out vehicle is a close company (basically one under the control of five or fewer persons).

Exhibit 2 sets out a more elaborate form of funding under which a bank, B, acquires the shares, and put and call options are entered into between the bank and T. T needs little funding until the option is exercised. In the meantime, B receives franked investment income in the form of dividends which are non-taxable in its hands. The funding cost is reflected in the price payable by T on exercise of the option, which is further reduced by the benefit derived by B from the dividend stream.

A simpler alternative is for the ESOP Trustee to acquire its shares on a partly paid basis, which would eliminate the need for the bulk of the funding until a later stage.

The Trustees of the ESOP could be individuals, such as the directors of the company, but it is usually preferable in the case of a UK ESOP to form a trustee subsidiary of the establishing company. This helps to avoid several potential traps under both company law and the Financial Services Act. Another advantage is that the formalities of changing directors of the trustee company are more straightforward than those required to change an individual trustee.

Exit routes for employees

An employee trust can itself provide an exit route for employee shareholders. In Exhibit 1, T is in a position to buy shares from employees using a combination of its bank facility and any other funds which may be available. The shares can then be sold to the APSS, and so effectively recycled time and again.

By way of a more elaborate exit, an internal market may be established in which employees may sell to one another in addition to, or instead of, dealing with an employee trust. Perhaps the most conspicuously successful internal market has been that of NFC, which operated for some years prior to the Company's flotation. Indeed, NFC's internal broker continues to operate to this day, even though there is a public market in NFC shares.

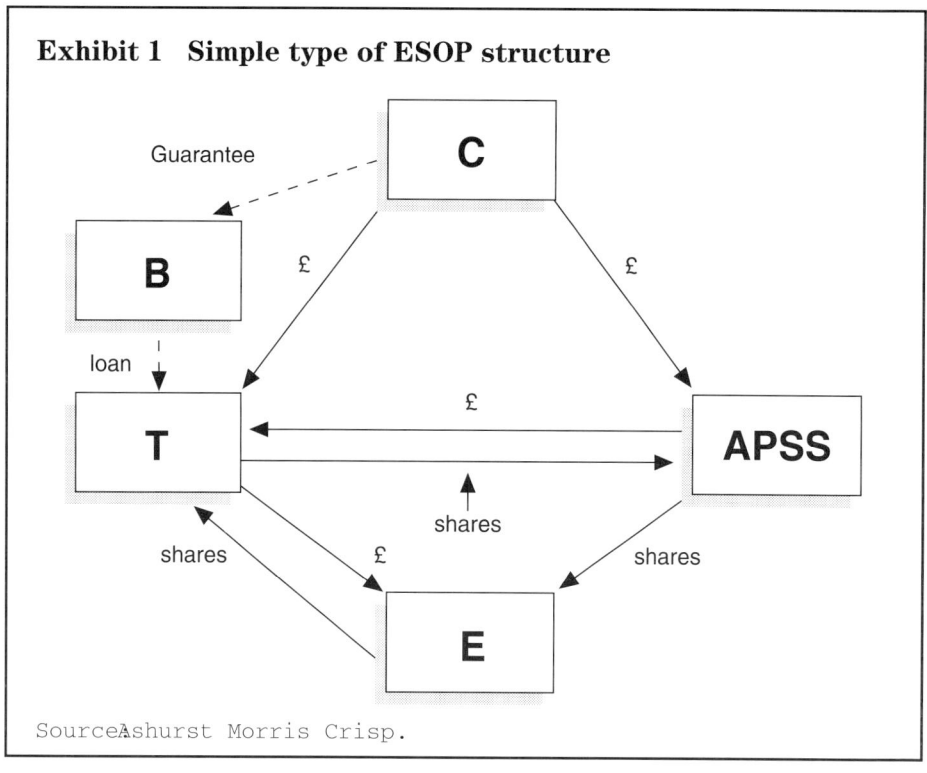

Exhibit 1   Simple type of ESOP structure

Source: Ashurst Morris Crisp.

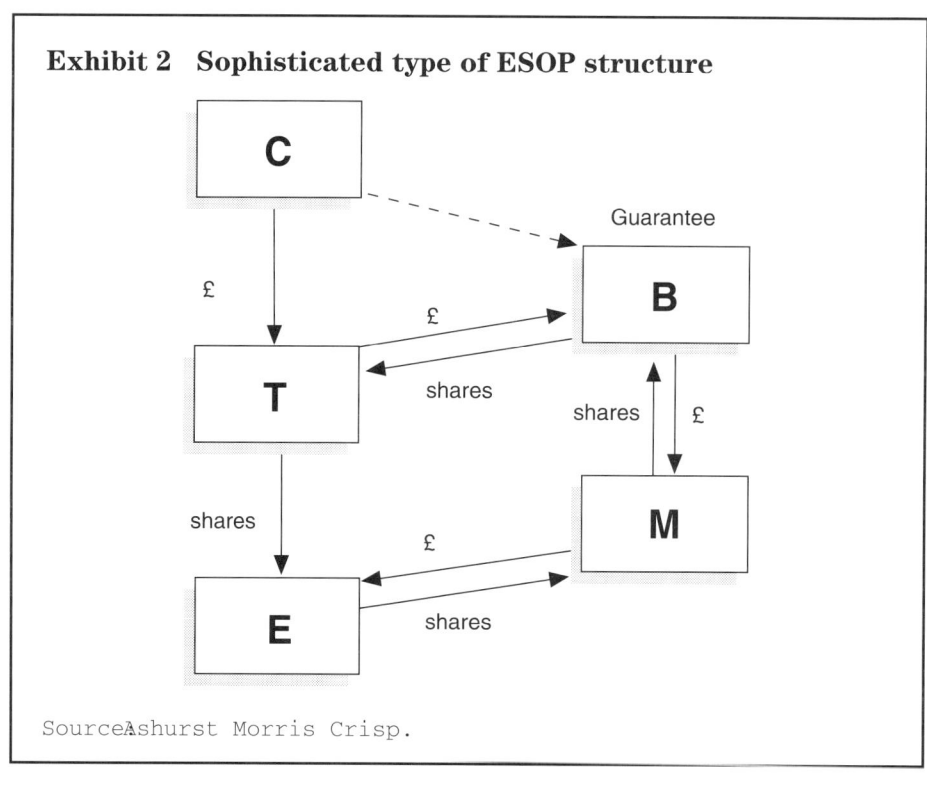

Exhibit 2   Sophisticated type of ESOP structure

Source: Ashurst Morris Crisp.

A number of unquoted companies have established internal markets under which there are regular dealing days on the basis of a formally determined price. Some, such as that of Harland & Wolff, have come about in the context of privatisations which have been effected by management/employee buy-outs.

Each internal market will be unique to its establishing company, but every such market requires one common feature in order to succeed: confidence. During the years before its flotation, NFC's shares showed a steady growth in value. The operation and presentation of the internal market created confidence in the shares. One market which failed did so because the shares were valued on the basis of supply and demand. Unless a company is insolvent, its shares, even if unquoted, have a value. An internal market inevitably rests on a very much smaller base of potential buyers and sellers. On a pure supply and demand basis, if on a particular dealing day there are ten sellers and no buyers, then the value of a share is by definition nil. Such a valuation cannot possibly create any confidence in the market.

Planning

Whatever route is to be followed in a particular buy-out, the question of management equity will be an issue from the outset. So, too, should that of employee equity involvement, since it is likely to impinge, in one way or another, on all the key aspects and documents of the buy-out. Quite apart from the share scheme itself, the articles of association of the buy-out vehicle, the shareholders agreement and, in some cases, the banking documentation and facilities must be considered, and appropriate provision made. The issues are not ones which may easily be left to the end of the negotiations.

8

Insurance

In recent years buy out teams have become increasingly conscious of the risks being taken by them. Effective due diligence undertaken by an experienced Insurance Broker will highlight specific areas of exposure and will recommend transfer to a correctly structured insurance programme.

This chapter will concentrate on the main areas of risk in a Buy Out situation:-

– Directors and Officers Liability;
– Environmental Impairment Liability;
– Warranty and Indemnity;
– Intellectual Property; and
– General Insurance.

Directors and Officers Liability Insurance

Directors, both executive and non-executive, are now reluctant to assume positions without the comfort of insurance protection. Until recently, few insurers provided appropriate cover but insurers are now prepared to underwrite policies adequately encompassing risk.

Risk arises in several forms; from allegations of breach of statutory duties (of which there are many) or from a breach of common law duties. Insurers agree to meet risk in the form of 'Wrongful Act'. It is imperative to ensure that 'Wrongful Act' is defined on a wide basis to include 'actual or alleged misfeasance, fraudulent or wrongful trading, breach of trust, breach of warranty or authority, breach of duty, neglect error or omissions, mis-statement, misleading statement or other acts wrongfully committed or attempted or any matter claimed against (them) solely by reason of (their) capacities as Directors or Officers; shadow or otherwise'.

If the policy is effectively underwritten to meet 'Wrongful Act' it will meet 'Loss' including 'such sums as the insured are legally liable to pay for reason of any wrongful act including awards of damages and costs made against the insured together with any legal costs, charges and expenses incurred by the insured in the defence of any legal action that is commenced or threatened in a court of civil or criminal jurisdiction at first instance or an appeal'. Underwriters will, however, exclude fines, penalties, punitive or exemplary damages and other specific areas as being uninsured.

One prominent insurer, AIG Europe (UK) Ltd now insists upon specific cover for 'employees'; in a Buy-Out situation it is important to ascertain that all management are protected. For example, a commonly cited source of Directors and Officers Liability claim is that of Health and Safety at Work Legislation. An employee may sustain an industrial injury on site and the Health and Safety Executive can prosecute the Board or individual site managers. Without taking prior cognisance of scope of insurance protection site managers may not be protected.

Also, insurers may exclude claims arising from action or inaction prior to the purchase of insurance. In an MBO situation the team must protect themselves from the outset of discussions; it is suggested that cover purchased carries a 'retroactive date' corresponding with the formation of the business plan.

Some exceptions to Directors' and Officers' Liability cover cannot be overridden with management teams ultimately meeting the cost of defence of civil claim or legal proceedings arising from:-

- loss of, or destruction of, or damage to, any material property;
- the breach, or alleged breach, of any professional duty owned other than in (their) capacity as a Directors or Officers of the Company;
- personal guarantees or indemnities; and
- seepage, pollution or contamination of any kind (actual or alleged).

Some such risks may be assumed by other Insurers to be discussed in detail later in this chapter.

In deciding that Directors' and Officers' Liability Insurance is required the management team must then determine the amount of cover to be purchased to provide adequate protection. Limits of indemnity are available on an 'aggregate basis' only and therefore consideration must be given to the maximum exposure in any one policy period.

Brokers should be approached early in negotiations to ensure availability of cover.

Professional Indemnity Insurance

As stated above, Directors' and Officers' Liability Insurance excludes claims for breach of professional duty - if advice is delivered for a fee that activities of the buy-out company can be protected by means of a Professional Indemnity policy.

Environmental Impairment Liability Insurance

Again, as stated above, underwriters are anxious to avoid liabilities in terms of the Environmental Protection Act 1990 and other legislation; to do so they impose almost 'blanket' exclusion of pollution and contamination. This exclusion requires careful study if the managerial team intend to be involved in any manufacturing process or supply of environmental products or services.

The asset base of the company itself could be prejudiced in the event of a loss and therefore the management team should consider protecting its investment by way of an 'environmental impairment liability coverage'.

Providers of such insurance are still limited but scope of cover is now improving with underwriters open to persuasion on certain risks. Cover continues, however, to be provided only subsequent to an environmental audit met at the cost of the client. Underwriters will not protect pre-existing contamination and will continue to impose a retroactive date of 'inception' effectively to guard against this. Underwriters have not yet revised their capacity for cover and continue to restrict their exposure by imposing high levels of self-insured deductibles and low levels of indemnity on an aggregate basis.

The very availability of cover, however limited, does merit consideration as part of due diligence.

Warranty and Indemnity Insurance

Faced with specific exclusions on Directors' and Officers' Liability policy the management team could look to the Warranty and Indemnity insurance market for a solution.

Specialist insurers will provide indemnity for 'damages' and costs and any warranty proceedings brought against a company's directors, parent company or shareholders as a result of the sale of their business assets. Detailed information is required by underwriters and will be assessed by their solicitors at a fee to be met by the management team.

Intellectual Property Rights Insurance

Cover can be made available to management teams and should be considered to protect patent applications or granted patents, copyrights, design rights, registered design, trademarks, service marks, brand names, logos or devices.

Cover is becoming ever more restrictive with limits of indemnity of £250,000 imposed as maximum. North American protection is also becoming difficult to obtain. Nevertheless cover can still be worthwhile as a means of meeting legal defence costs arising from infringement or alleged infringement.

Again, many issues need to be addressed by management teams and close liaison with brokers is strongly recommended. Some of the key areas to consider are:

Material Damage

In most commercial situations, the management team will require cover for buildings, machinery, plant and stock. In addition to these areas it may be necessary to arrange cover for property while it is still being built. This form of cover is known as 'Contractor's All Risks'.

The insurance company will require the management to identify at the outset the perils which they are insuring. The standard fire policy cover extends to fire, lightning, explosion, storm, tempest or flood, burst pipes, earthquake, aircraft, riot, civil commotion, malicious damage, explosion and impact. It is now possible to purchase additional coverage in the form of Accidental Damage, which enhances the basic coverage. It is also normal for companies to insure their property against the risk of theft.

Business Interruption

This class of insurance will cover any loss of profits, or the additional expenses necessary, after some element of physical property is damaged. The Material Damage policy already mentioned insures the value of the property damaged or destroyed, but not the losses arising from the reduction in turnover during the repair period. Again, this is an imperative protection for the buy-out team.

The most common interruption policies are those which cover losses resulting from:

– fire and special perils;
– engineering breakdown; and
– computer damage and breakdown.

Employers Liability Insurance

Where an employee is injured because of the fault of the employer, the injured person can claim compensation or 'damages' from the employer. Compulsory insurance is subject to the Employers' Liability (Compulsory Insurance) Act 1969, which has been effective from 1 January 1972. The compulsory policy covers legal liability for bodily injury, illness or disease of employees arising out of, or in the course of, the business. The management team is legally obliged to protect the interest of the workforce.

The question of employees working off-shore is of particular concern following the Piper Alpha disaster. Following upon this, all Employers' Liability Insurance policies specifically exclude work on off-shore installations, unless this has been agreed with the underwriters. There is normally a limit on this cover of £2 million. Previously all other contingencies were 'unlimited' in amount but a limit of £10 million is now imposed.

Public Liability

Members of the public may suffer injury or damage to their property due to the activities of someone else, and the Public Liability Insurances are designed to provide compensation for those who may have to pay damages or legal costs for such injuries, or for damage to property. There are specific exclusions of damage or injury arising out of products sold or supplied for which there is a specific extension to policies. Whilst it is not actually compulsory, no management team should attempt to run a business without adequate public liability protection.

Products Liability Insurance

This can be a very onerous liability for a management team involved in manufacturing processes, and it is one that the majority of insurers prefer to deal with separately. If a person is injured by any product he or she purchases, and can show that the seller - or, in some cases, the manufacturer - was to blame, then they could succeed in a claim for damages.

The standard policy provides coverage for liability arising out of goods sold, or supplied, that cause bodily injury, illness or disease of third party persons, or loss of, or damage to, third party property. Varying limits of indemnity can be obtained, dependent upon the risks to which underwriters are exposed.

Motor Vehicle Insurance

This should insure the business for damage to vehicles, but should also cover any legal liability in respect of damage to third party property or persons.

Marine Cargo

Cargo is usually insured on a warehouse-to-warehouse basis, frequently covering All Risks. Cover is dependent upon the mode of transport and the responsibilities accepted by the company.

Engineering Insurance

With the increasing sophistication of machinery and plant, there are a number of risks which can be insured:-

(a) statutory inspection (obligatory for certain types of plant);
(b) damage to, or breakdown of, specific items of plant and machinery;
(c) cost of repair of own surrounding property due to (b);
(d) legal liability for injury caused by (b);
(e) legal liability for damage to property of others caused by (b);
(f) loss of profits due to breakdown of key items of plant.

Credit Insurance

Traders can sustain heavy losses by reason of insolvency or protracted default on the part of buyers of their goods. Credit insurance can provide protection against this; it may be used to insure against losses arising from both United Kingdom and overseas buyers.

Legal expenses Insurance

Cover is available against the ever-increasing possibility of legal action.

Terrorism Damage

Following the recent bomb outrages in London, all insurance companies now restrict terrorism damage cover to £100,000 in respect of each loss pertaining to property damage, business interruption and computer insurance. However, it is possible to buy cover from the new insurer 'Pool Re' - an insurer which was set up by the various insurance companies specifically to carry the terrorism risk.

Certain discussions are underway as regards the feasibility or otherwise of the 'Pool Re' arrangement. Rates vary according to geographical area and post code, with the most expensive rates being in central London and the metropolitan areas of Manchester, Birmingham, Leeds, Glasgow, Edinburgh etc.

Insurance Premium Tax

Since 1 October 1994 an amount of 2.5 per cent is levied on all insurance premiums and remitted to the Revenue. Such amounts must be included in any management team budgets.

Life after the buy-out

"Mark this, ye proud men of action"
H Heine
German 19th c. poet

Achieving a management buy-out is probably the most stressful and rewarding undertaking that most managers can undertake. At the moment of signing the contract they will have fulfilled a dream - never mind that it is at the cost of mortgaging the family assets. But once the feeling of euphoria has passed, to be replaced by the normal fears and uncertainties of day to day management, how do they face up to the next set of challenges?

Management teams from all walks of life, and in all sizes of companies, can gain the opportunity to become shareholders in their own businesses. But whether they are managing a $500 million subsidiary or a multi-national company, or a $1 million private company for a retiring shareholder, they will face common problems. Before diving back into the day to day decision-making routine of managing a business, it is worth making time available to consider the implications of independence. This chapter identifies some of the issues which most buy-out teams will be forced to confront, and provides some guidelines which may help to resolve them. These guidelines are not necessarily from the management text books, but are based on several years of experience in funding buy-outs and in helping management teams to make a success of their venture.

The first year

Understanding your backers

There is one feature common to all buy-outs: the business is under new ownership. The larger the transaction, the greater the likelihood that the business will be majority-owned by the institutional financiers. Change of ownership and control brings new and unique problems. The principal one is that, to the institutions, the company's main function is to provide a high, relatively short-term return on their investment. This is most unlike being owned by a corporate. The corporate shareholder can have a very different perspective: expectations of returns on equity are significantly different; the business or division is viewed within the context of a broader strategic plan; and investment decisions, whether in assets or R&D, are taken within a group context. The change of ownership has consequences in respect of financial reporting, career development for junior and middle management and employee relationships.

The new owner or partner will not have had time to develop a thorough and detailed understanding of the business, although if management have chosen well they will work to build-up their understanding as time progresses. (Buy-out teams have a tendency to complain that their backers do not understand the business; or that they demand too much information; or waste management time.) Furthermore, as we have seen in earlier chapters, institutions will have negotiated rights to control fundamental aspects of the business. They do this principally in order to protect their investment, as minority partners. Management will find themselves subject to detailed contracts of employment, and their hands will be tied in many strategic areas. For example, it is most unlikely that management can sell 'key' assets, hire or fire senior staff, make acquisitions or disposals, or enter into a large capital-expenditure programme, without obtaining the consent of either the investor's non-executive director or the institution itself. Total independence is illusory. As a new buy-out manager, you have to recognise this and learn to deal with it.

All of this means that your relationships with your backers have to be managed. The following pointers and questions may be useful:

- Understand and relate to their objectives;
- What is their time scale to realisation? Your business goals will have to fit in with their time scale;
- What is their house style, and their corporate culture? Can you live with it?
- Are they experienced in your industry? If not, include an induction programme to help them develop an in-depth knowledge;
- Understand and manage their information requirements; and
- Try to develop a close personal, as well as a business, relationship. Personality clashes are not conducive to good performance.

All investors know of several management teams who find their 'interference' and demands tiresome and irksome. If you adopt this attitude, you will eventually regret it. Your backers can hold the key to future success – they are a business resource that has to be managed and developed. It is important to build upon the relationships established at the time of the transaction.

Communication
Immediately after the buy-out, it is important to communicate to your staff, customers and suppliers exactly what the implications of the change of ownership

are likely to mean. As with your backers, the key is building relationships and confidence. In practice, of course, there may be very few changes, but people will need to be spoken to and the new ownership explained. There are a number of well-known cases where a failure to communicate has led to a loss of key staff and customers.

Employees

This may be stating the obvious, but talking and explaining the buy-out to your company's employees is critical. Knowledge of the deal may be in the public domain, or you may have had to negotiate in secrecy. Whichever, rumours and snippets of information will have gone around your offices and the factory floor – leading to fear and uncertainty. So, as soon as you can, explain the deal! A buy-out should give a significant boost to company morale – it clears uncertainty and should give all your staff more confidence.

A buy-out should be seen as a new beginning. Major changes can be made – changes that were previously thought of as impossible or very difficult. Exploit the opportunity that the buy-out creates. But the management team needs the loyalty and support of the workforce, so prepare a communication strategy for the immediate period after the buy-out and for the future. Make sure that communication becomes a habit and a part of the corporate culture.

You may find that there are special difficulties with managers and staff that were excluded from the buy-out team. Jealousy and resentment may well be their first emotional response. Creating a climate for motivation may well become critical, so the team and the backers should already have considered employee share schemes and other incentives. Act on this quickly – management will need support, and it is important that all staff should feel that they are part of the team.

Customers and suppliers

As with your employees, the news of a buy-out can create both positive and negative attitudes in your customers and suppliers. You will need their support and confidence, so be prepared to spend time explaining the deal and your future strategy. Meanwhile, your competitors may be trying to take advantage of the uncertainty that a buy-out can create. Sometimes, a buy-out will be viewed sympathetically by suppliers and customers. This may even lead to opportunities to re-negotiate prices, credit terms and service levels.

Conversely, beware of the opposite. Customers may seek to cancel contracts, through exercising break-clauses arising from the change of ownership. Some will almost inevitably try to squeeze better terms from you.

So, in summary:

– Communicate and explain;
– Anticipate customer and competitor reactions;
– Plan for adversity; and
– Exploit the opportunity to obtain improved terms.

Include in your communication strategy the leading credit agencies. Your own credit-rating is something to be closely monitored, and it can have an important influence on the terms that may be negotiated with most suppliers. It is quite likely that your company's rating was affected by the financial health of your former corporate owner (for better or worse). Manage and try to influence the change of circumstances following the buy-out.

Finally, public relations are important, and are often badly handled by newly independent managements. A public relations plan should form part of your communications strategy – avoid issuing rushed and poorly drafted press releases. In planning how to present the new company's image to points of contact with the outside world, it is advisable to appoint a PR consultant (preferably well before the deal is announced).

Creating a corporate culture
Why is it that so many buy-outs enjoy a significant improvement in profitability in the first year or two following the change of ownership? More often than not, the improvement can be put down to a combination of the release of entrepreneurial talent and the motivation brought about through ownership. Costs and overheads that were thought to be critical to a company's performance are found to be a luxury. Moreover, research carried out by the stockbroker James Capel has shown that, despite some notable failures in 1994, MBOs tend to perform better after being floated on the Stock Exchange than other new issues. This clearly suggests that the improvements achieved by an MBO are not just short term.

The psychological effect of ownership is interesting. Managers and employees suddenly develop an acute sense of proprietorship, but through this the business culture can become one of risk aversion. This is not surprising, and to an extent can be beneficial. Nonetheless, the buy-out backers will be looking for entrepreneurial flair within the management team. This may not be the initial source of equity added-value – fancy footwork on structuring the deal can do wonders for equity returns – but if your objective is to build a business with a long-term future, you will need the entrepreneurial approach to penetrate and to become the core of the business's culture.

This culture should be created in the boardroom. The styles and attitudes adopted at this level help to mould the organisation's ethos. It is important that managers understand and actively develop the style that they perceive to be right for the organisation. Like all the resources available to the business, corporate culture should be managed.

Rationalisation

In the early 90's many buy-out opportunities arose as a result of parent company rationalisation. Either because of pressure from banks, shareholders or, in some cases, holding company directors actually taking the initiative to refocus a group's strategy, cash was required centrally. This often meant that cash had been stripped out of subsidiaries, leading to shortage of investment funds and difficulty in financing working capital. Management may have started to respond to parent company financial demands through cash saving and generation actions. However, the buy-out opportunity of greater control enables management to adopt a more positive and aggressive attitude in implementing its own rationalisation programme. More often than not, the business plan submitted to financiers contains overhead savings and other margin improvement measures. However, the organisational changes in which responsibilities for various courses of action are allocated have not been considered in detail, because of time constraints in the MBO planning process and senior management being involved in the deal rather than dedicated to operational measures. It is important, therefore, that the newly independent management works quickly to implement change.

IMPLEMENTING CHANGE

– Set objectives.

– Define responsibilities.

– Agree the detailed measures.

– Communicate.

– Control, through effective information flows.

– Incentivise and motivate staff.

Privatisation

A management or employee buy-out of a non-private sector business presents different and additional challenges to the management team and its backers. However, by the time the management and employees have won the backing of venture capitalists, many of the parameters for establishing a profit-orientated business will have been established.

The one advantage of most privatisations is that management is given more time (and often financial help in obtaining advice) to create a business plan. As privatisations are now well established, the vendor agencies normally have the experience to implement many of the required organisational changes required for a successful privatisation. Nonetheless, many, if not all, of the management team and key supervisory staff will not have the experience of working in a profit motivated organisation. Business plan preparation, how to find backers and advisors are topics covered elsewhere in this book. One point worth emphasising, however, is the importance of finding an experienced 'chairman-designate' to work with management at the planning stage. Bringing such an individual into the team not only helps in conducting negotiations with the vendor agency but should strengthen the development of a new business culture within the business.

A common feature of many privatisations is that the customer for the service initially remains the same. For example, a privatised council agency, for refuse collection or property maintenance will still be selling its service to the local authority. Such agencies may be given a local monopoly for a period of time but eventually will be forced to compete, either for contract renewal or against other companies prepared to offer a competing parallel service (as has happened in the bus industry). This breathing space must be used to broaden the customer base, improve productivity and service levels. The implication for the organisation can be dramatic so the ability of management to handle change in all aspects of the organisation will be tested right at the outset.

Dealing with difficulties

Buy-outs can go wrong. Poor management is a common reason, but sheer bad luck can also play its part. Also, the funding structures used to create the buy-out often have a bearing on success or failure. It is quite possible to have a well-managed, even profitable business, which is ruined by the ill-advised high gearing that was created when the business was bought out.

WARNING SIGNS
- Recessionary economic environment. An overview of the economic environment should form part of your annual budgetary procedures.

- Market changes. Ideally, you should be influencing the development of the markets for the company's products or services. However, threats can creep up, such as competitor discounting or import penetration; work out a strategic response to these changes.

- Cash flow. Ideally, cash flow should be monitored weekly and forecasts rolled forward as part of a dynamic planning process. A tightening of cash flow can result from lower than budgeted margins, weak credit control or ineffective control over costs (trading or capital expenditure). Monitor bank covenants: even profitable, cash-generative businesses can breach covenants if these are set too tight.

- Reducing book-to-bill ratios. This management tool is commonly used in the United States, but not so often in Europe. A declining level of contract bookings compared to sales is a sure indicator of trouble; a lower ratio may result from an increase in failed tenders or a straight forward decline in customer activity. The earlier this weakness is picked-up, and its cause identified, the more time you have to take effective management action.

- Z-chart analysis. A number of companies use this tool to keep track of longer-term trends in the business. It can be a useful way to present data and an aid to help management understand the dynamics of its business.

Early symptoms

The best way to manage a crisis is to anticipate that crisis. The earlier the warning signals are picked up, the longer a company has to take corrective action and to maintain the confidence of bankers and institutional shareholders. Warning signs are always easier to spot with hindsight, but the list given in the adjacent panel may help to develop a management strategy for dealing with impending difficulties.

Strain in a business can be detected in many ways other than those suggested in the panel. For example, communication breakdown between managers, declining customer service, production inefficiencies and so on. Whatever the cause, sooner or later the effects will show up in the business's cash flow.

Cash-flow crisis

A cash-flow crisis implies a certain degree of management failure. Nonetheless, many buy-outs at some stage go through a cash-flow crisis. It may not be trading related per se. Debt-repayment obligations can fall due at the most inconvenient times in the course of business development. Many buy-outs in the late 1980s were completed on the assumption that the economy would continue to grow. Thus the recession of the early 90's led to many breaches of banking covenants, failure to repay debt on schedule, and consequential restructuring or receivership. Management, bankers and venture capitalists alike failed to read the warning signals, and had to deal with difficult situations. However, although some buy-outs ended up in receivership, many of those which got into difficulty have survived. Indeed, a number of successful stock-market flotations during 1993 and 1994 were of buy-out companies which went through some form of financial restructuring. The stock-market route can actually be part of this restructuring process, when equity is raised to reduce debt.

So how does management deal with a cash-flow crisis? More often than not, the answer is confidence. The worst thing that can happen is to spring surprises on the backers. Confidence will be developed from the communication strategy talked about earlier. Management must keep their bankers and equity partners informed. Give them time to react and to work together to resolve the problems. There is no point in approaching a bank a few days before the company is about to breach a facility level or an important covenant. Banks and venture capitalists do not like to have to make decisions in an atmosphere of crisis and pressure. So the earlier that they are made aware of the difficulties, the better the chance of reaching a positive and constructive solution.

Make use of the non-executive director representative that institutions often have on the board. Most non-executives will become a strong ally of management after some time on the board. Even if they retain their independence from executive management, they will identify themselves with the success or failure of a company. Properly used, the non-executive can be an important ingredient in convincing the backers that the venture is worth supporting.

Backers will always be impressed with early management action to deal with trading problems. A confident management style, reflected in taking the tough decisions in good time, will normally help retain the loyalty and support of the financial partners. Half-hearted attempts to reduce costs or to develop new markets at the instigation of non-executives will not. Show strong leadership – the backers will often look to be led themselves. If management are seen to initiate the moves towards correcting the anticipated cash-flow difficulties, then the battle is half won.

Although crisis management will inevitably put a lot of strain and stress on individuals, try not to forget the overall objective of the whole venture. That is to make money! For the banker, it is important that the loans continue to be serviced and, however structured or restructured, that there remains a realistic prospect that debt will eventually be repaid. For the equity backer, the main objective will be to realise a capital profit through an exit, by way of a trade sale or a stock-market listing. Any strategy for dealing with a refinancing requirement must include, at its core, these objectives.

Realisation

If there is one certainty in the cycle of a buy-out, it is that the backers will, sooner or later, want to seek an exit. Why do most backers of buy-outs seemingly take a comparatively short-term view of their investments? The answer is quite simple. Venture funds typically raise their finance from institutional investors, such as pension funds, insurance companies or banks. These investors have many choices of investment, such as UK and overseas stock markets, gilts, bonds, property and cash. Each category attracts a portfolio risk weighting and, equally as important, an assessment of liquidity. Investors prefer liquid investments, as they can alter their portfolio category balances depending on their own cash needs (for paying pensioners or meeting insurance claims, for example). Investments in private companies, such as buy-outs, are illiquid – their shares are not easily traded. The price extracted by institutions is the possibility (indeed, probability) of a high rate of return and a short exit horizon. Another characteristic of the venture capital industry, a direct result of the need for institutional liquidity, is that most funds are established as limited-life vehicles. These may be limited partnerships or investment trusts, typically having a life of ten years. The reward basis for venture capitalists is often based on fund performance – and a venture fund manager would find it difficult to raise new money if after ten years the fund portfolio was still full of unsold investments.

Exit, of course, is not only about the requirements for the investor. Management and employees participating in equity incentive schemes will, sooner or later, wish to realise their paper participations for hard cash or more liquid securities. Personal needs, retirement or security are all good reasons for wanting to sell shares. Many financing structures of buy-outs include the ubiquitous ratchet, which, on achievement of a profit or company value target, will give management shareholders a bigger reward. So, from Day One, the pressure is on to achieve the exit.

Finally, and not least, there is the business strategy. Most companies will at some time need to raise new capital to maintain growth, to survive or to redeem debt. Capital raising, whether through the stock market or by the introduction of a new investor, may create opportunities for the selling of shares.

Timing

Timing of the exit is critical to wealth and return maximisation. However, objectives of institutional shareholders and managers/employees commonly will be different, leading to different priorities in both timing and choice of exit route. Many venture funds are measured on the percentage internal rate of return (IRR) achieved. Cash generated is important but not necessarily the prime measure. A venture fund's own investors will be impressed with a net return of say 15 per cent over the FT All-share index; the IRR achieved is a simple way of comparing one venture funds performance against another. Thus if after two or three years, management's investor could realise a 35 per cent IRR, but the prospect for the next two or three years reduce expectations to a 25 per cent IRR, management may well come under pressure to acceed to an early sale, even if strategically or personally such a sale is premature. How do they deal with this? Firstly, they try to convince their backers that competitive returns will still be achieved. Secondly, as talked about in the next section, management may be able to find another backer to buy the stake held by the original backer(s).

Hopefully, management will have found backing from more pragmatic investors; exit timing then becomes more of a function of considerations of economic conditions, the characteristics of the business itself and strategy.

Market/economic conditions

The economic cycle is the major influence determining exit values and getting timing right in relation to the cycle is critical. Overlaying the economic cycle are trends in the stockmarket and trends in the company's own market. Not all will co-incide. For example, the engineering sector tends to be a leading indicator, business services a lagging indicator. Unless the company has non cyclical characteristics, it seems logical that the optimum time for maximising value is between mid cycle and towards the top.

Management should also consider what it is about the business that is likely to make it attractive to a buyer or to the stock market. For example is it a mature business, secure in its market but slow growing? Exit timing for this sort of business will be cycle driven. If the business is growing strongly timing may be determined by the cash needs of the business, profit performance being more important than the general macro market considerations. Growth by acquisition may well best be achieved by obtaining a stock market listing at the same time – presenting an exit opportunity for some of the shareholders. Whatever management's business strategy, the key point is that an exit strategy for their venture or the private equity backers has to be agreed before the deal is consummated and that as time goes by, exit moves towards the top of the agenda.

Deciding on an exit route

Many different factors will contribute to the choice of exit route. "Exit" is a term that is loosely used by venture capitalists; for them, it is the opportunity to realise their whole investment, but it does not necessarily mean that the shareholders will sell out – it can mean providing the opportunity to sell shares, through a stock-market listing. Management shareholders may choose to retain all, or a substantial holding of, their shares in the expectation of longer-term capital growth. The four main exit routes are discussed in some detail below but, of course, variations are possible – for example, the institutional backers can sell their holding to a corporate buyer who may be seeking a joint venture. In some circumstances, the corporate buyer may wish management and employees to retain all or part of their shares as part of an incentive scheme.

The stock-market listing

Many management teams set their hearts on the stock-market route. More often than not, the initial thinking is that a share listing provides a market for the institutional backers' shares, whilst leaving management in control of its own destiny. However, the fundamental purpose of the market is to obtain access to new capital at a price which minimises the dilution of the existing shareholders' interests. New capital can be used for acquisitions, or, more likely in the case of a buy-out, to redeem debt and preference shares.

The detailed criteria that a company will normally have to comply with to meet stock-market listing requirements can be obtained from the Stock Exchange brokers or advisers. When deciding whether or not their company is a suitable candidate for listing, the management should ask whether their company has:

- a realistic strategy for growth,
- critical mass in the company's markets,
- a professional management team, and
- capitalisation in excess of £25 million.

Stock-market investors will look for the above in nearly all new listings. Although small companies are now back in fashion, it is noticeable that most recent floats have achieved a market capitalisation in excess of £50 million. However, following the decision to close the USM in 1996, the Stock Exchange has announced proposals for an Alternative Investment Market. The objective of this initiative is to allow smaller companies to access an alternative source of capital and to provide a market for shares for companies unable to access the Official List. Companies whose shares are currently traded under Rule 4.2 will transfer to the new market. Listing requirements will be significantly less stringent than the Official List although trading will be subject to similar levels of supervision. This new market will be suitable for small companies, probably with higher risk profiles than companies normally accepted onto the Official List. Management will need to consider very carefully the implications of joining such a market.

One possible route into the market for companies that do not fulfil the criteria listed above, may be through a 'reverse take-over' of an existing quoted company. There are literally hundreds of companies with a capitalisation of less than £20 million. Some are leftovers from the heyday of the USM, or previous new-issue booms, and are still trading. Others are literally 'shells' – companies for which the quote is the main asset, with perhaps a small cash balance. Investors in these companies are, to all intents and purposes, trapped in an extremely illiquid vehicle, and may be responsive to any bright ideas suggested by the progressive management of a small company.

Managements that believe that listing is the most appropriate route to follow may meet resistance from their institutional backers. Venture funds, whatever their nature, often prefer a clean exit in the form of a cash consideration from a trade buyer. Indeed, the possibility of seeking a listing is something that should be raised during the selection of investors; sponsors are now used to dealing with venture funds, so this problem can be resolved.

Obtaining a quote on the stock market is expensive and time consuming. Management will be thrown into the limelight and will find it quite a testing process. Before making the commitment, managements should ensure that a task force is established to organise the whole process. Its tasks will include:

– preparation of a new strategic plan,
– proposals for restructuring the board,
– selection of a broker, merchant bank and other advisers,
– liaison with institutional shareholders and employee shareholder groups,
– renegotiation of banking facilities, term-debt arrangements, and discussions with the holders of other securities (preference shareholders, mezzanine holders, etc.),
– publicity and PR, and
– presentation and marketing packs for presentations to new potential shareholders.

Once advisers have been selected, the list of things to do expands alarmingly. A good adviser will lead the management through the process efficiently and with any luck make the whole task enjoyable. So be careful and take your time when selecting an adviser – always try to meet a selection of advisers before making your choice.

It is important to sort out the board membership before you float. The appointment of a new chairman who has City experience and credibility can add a lot of value to the new issue price. Also, you will need to ensure that there are a further two non-executive directors on the Board (to meet the Cadbury Report recommendations).

Finally, a word about investor relations. The road from private to public company can be quite straightforward. However, one of the most significant changes will be in the management's relationship with its backers. It is probable that it will lose its original backer's non-executive director, and thus will lose a day-to-day point of contact. It is important, however, to create a good working relationship with the new shareholders – management will need their support in the future.

The trade sale

Trade sales are the most common form of exit from buy-outs. This is largely due to the fact that most buy-outs are of relatively small companies, unsuitable for the Stock Market. Trade sales can form part of a planned strategy, agreed at the time of the buy-out. More commonly, the strategy is superseded by opportunism (an unsolicited offer out of the blue), or by necessity, if the company gets into trouble.

Selecting a buyer

How do management and institutional shareholders go about selecting the 'best' purchaser of the company? The first thing to note is that, in most circumstances, management has the 'whip-hand'. Acquirers would normally be reluctant to proceed with a purchase without the support and agreement of the incumbent management. Nonetheless, to avoid the painful process of falling out with its backers, management should endeavour to reach an agreement on the exit strategy. They must try to obtain a consensus, both within management and amongst backers, on how the whole exercise should be managed.

Clearly, an individual company's circumstances will tend to form the core constituent of the exit strategy. Whatever these circumstances may be, unless management is responding to an opportunistic approach, the most appropriate way of dealing with exit is to appoint an independent corporate adviser.

The benefits of this approach are:

– a professional and experienced framework within which to conduct the sale process,
– effective use of management time,
– tactical considerations in price and term negotiations,
– resolving conflict between shareholders,
– possibility of lateral thinking approach to identifying potential acquirers, and
– advice on sensitive information disclosure, due diligence and contractual requirements.

Backers will be able to help in advisor selection. However, the final decision should rest with the management, as it is they who will spend most time in the negotiation process. Management will undoubtedly have thought about possible acquirers. Indeed, it is quite feasible to 'position' the company in its marketplace with a view to selling out to an identified buyer. The important thing is that all parties should feel happy with the outcome. Each party should have defined its expectations prior to entering into negotiations, so that there is an initial strategy against which the outcome of each decision in the disposal process may be measured.

Share repurchase

Using this mechanism as an exit route is relatively uncommon, because it is difficult to persuade the institutional backers that they are achieving the optimal rate of return on investment. It can work where:

– the company is cash rich and has built up high distributable reserves,

- management are very keen to retain independence,
- the company is not big enough to be floated on the Stock Exchange, and
- a small minority of institutions wish to exit, the majority are prepared to stay in.

The Companies Act lays down tight rules for share repurchases, so professional advice needs to be sought before this exit route is seriously considered.

Refinancing

It is becoming increasingly common for a management to execute a second buy-out, replacing the original backer with new investors. In a sense, this type of transaction recognises the strength of the management's negotiating position. A refinancing opportunity may arise when:

- management and backers fall out or have a fundamental disagreement on strategy,
- the original backer's fund runs out of time and is forced to exit, and
- there is scope to re-leverage the company, giving original backers an exit opportunity and replacing them with new investors who are prepared to accept a higher level of risk.

Due to the prolonged recession, quite a number of venture capital funds are reaching the end of their fixed lives. To preserve their own credibility in fund raising, they will have to realise their remaining portfolio holdings. Nonetheless, these investments may be relatively sound companies, just beginning to emerge from the recession, and may be quite "backable". Once again, it is important to appoint an external adviser, who can help resolve pricing and conflicts of interest issues, as well as assisting in finding new backers. Management and employee shareholders may also have the opportunity to sell shares, and new management shareholders can be included in new incentive arrangements.

Common problems

The issues discussed below almost invariably feature in the disposal of an institution-backed buy-out.

Institutional warranties

Management should be aware that most institutions will not provide warranties on a disposal; this applies to both a stock-market listing and to a trade sale. The conundrum to resolve is that, not only do institutions not give warranties, they will require the same terms of consideration as the management.

Cash or shares

It cannot be recommended strongly enough that at least part of the consideration should be taken in cash – unless the sale is a forced one in adverse circumstances. Many vendors or companies in the late 1980s took shares in the acquirer as consideration, only to find that they were virtually unsaleable, or that the value had dropped, when recession struck; in some cases, when the high-flyer purchaser went bust, the shares were worth nothing at all.

Continuing motivation

Following a successful disposal, senior management participants in the original buy-out may become very wealthy. This, of course, was one of the main objects of the exercise. However, to ensure the continuing success of the business, even under new ownership, these managers must be prepared to share some of their success. For example, they should consider negotiating an attractive incentive scheme for their staff, and they should carefully plan for the management succession.

Concluding remarks

As with the original buy-out deal, exiting can be an emotional and testing experience. The manager will again have to deal with conflicts of interest, resolve the concerns of employees, negotiate very complex issues with the institutional investors, and so on. A good, independent non-executive chairman and non-executive director should be able to take some of the pressure off the management and investor representatives. In addition, the appointment of an outside corporate finance adviser is something that should be seriously considered by all parties. It is important to be able to present a common negotiating stance to potential purchasers. Disagreement in the vendor camp will lead to a weak negotiating position, which a purchaser will undoubtedly exploit.

In a sense, we have gone a full circle. At the beginning of this chapter, the importance of investor relationships and of an agreement on business strategy was stressed. Following the buy-out, the relationship between the backers and the management will hopefully have strengthened. An effective use of non-executive directors will have helped to cement the relationships, and will have contributed to the development of a common corporate strategy.

The recession of the early 1990s has thrown up some interesting situations – situations in which both management and backers have had to reappraise their original objectives and act accordingly. It was very common in the boom years for all parties to agree, without a great deal of thought or contingency planning, that the main objective of the buy-out company was to float on the Stock Exchange or USM. Some companies managed to achieve a float after only a couple of years. Those buy-out companies which have survived the recession – and most have – have done so because the shareholders have worked together. The final test of the relationship comes when all parties sit down to agree a sale. The venture capitalist with broad shoulders can often be persuaded to ease the pain by offering new incentives. But remember, although the exit for the venture fund may be final, it will not be final for the management and the employees. Be it a marriage with the Stock Exchange and new institutional investors, or with a corporate buyer, it is still a new beginning – so choose your partner carefully!

10

Management buy-ins

A management buy-in (MBI) is a transaction in which a manager or team of managers from outside a particular company and their financial backers purchase equity control. In the process, the manager becomes chairman, chief executive or managing director, and gains a significant equity stake. In addition, during the early 1990s, we have seen the emergence of a powerful variant of MBIs – the 'MBIO' or 'BIMBO'. In this situation, a manager from outside, together with management from within the company, and their financial backers, purchase the company. BIMBOs often possess significant advantages over conventional MBIs, and these are described later in this chapter.

As Exhibit 1 shows, from 1985 the number of MBIs completed each year in the United Kingdom grew rapidly to a peak of almost 150 transactions in 1989. Along with most other merger and acquisitions activity, MBIs declined quite severely in 1990 and again in 1993. In the latter case this was principally due to a poor first half when confidence was hit by the UK's exit from the ERM mechanism. Anecdotally the market and the experience of 1994 suggests a consistent pick-up since.

In 1990 MBI managers and their backers became somewhat nervous of acquiring companies with rapidly softening earnings – particularly as the vendors tended to base their asking prices on the previous year's profits and price/earnings multiples. However, in 1991 the numbers of MBIs held steady, despite a further collapse in overall merger and acquisitions activity. This steady level of activity was probably due to the fact that, although the short-term outlook was bleak, certain investors and individuals took the view that if they could buy a profitable company at recessionary prices and manage that company more aggressively, then in the long term they would be in an advantageous position. Many of these investors have since felt that they moved slightly early, but now that the United Kingdom is out of recession at last, these could prove to have been well-timed deals.

What sort of people do MBIs?

In the UK, there are essentially two main types of buy-in manager: the 'break-out' manager and the 'second time entrepreneur'. Most institutions will have experience of MBIs. 3i have carried out detailed research into the MBI and their experience in France and Germany, where the markets are behind that of the UK in volume but nevertheless developing quite quickly, show that the profiles and motives of managers undertaking MBIs in those countries are remarkably similar.

The 'break-out' manager
The typical 'break-out' manager has a distinct profile:

– early to mid 40,
– divisional chief executive within larger corporate,
– five or more years of chief executive experience,
– about £100,000 to commit (the greater part of personal net worth),
– looking for a £5 million plus turnover business,
– has a good mixture of professionalism/discipline gained from a larger company, combined with an entrepreneurial approach gained from experience with a smaller company, and
– main difficulty will be finding a target company.

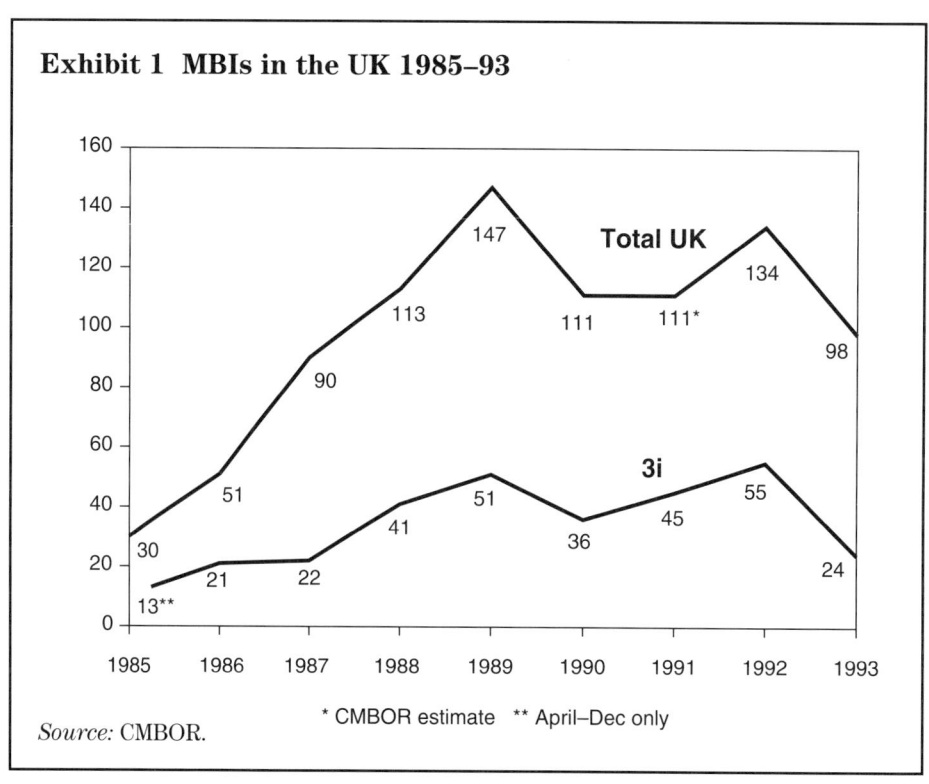

Exhibit 1 MBIs in the UK 1985–93

Total UK: 30, 51, 90, 113, 147, 111, 111*, 134, 98

3i: 13**, 21, 22, 41, 51, 36, 45, 55, 24

Years: 1985, 1986, 1987, 1988, 1989, 1990, 1991, 1992, 1993

* CMBOR estimate   ** April–Dec only

Source: CMBOR.

The 'break-out' manager usually has many motives for contemplating an MBI:

– wants independence,
– frustrated in current role through his career having become blocked, or maybe because the more senior roles have become unfulfilling and bureaucratic,
– cannot do an MBO as the business the manager runs is not for sale at a feasible price,
– wants to make significant capital, and
– may be a corporate victim, having been taken over, delayered or downsized (This is a potentially dangerous motive as well as a powerful one!).

The 'break-out' manager faces a number of common dangers. He may not be a suitable manager for the companies typically available, which are generally smaller than the 'break-out' manager has run. Often such managers have a strong operational background, which may mean weakness on the financial or acquisition aspects of the MBI. There is also the chance that the manager will overpay for the company if the search for a target has taken a long time.

The boss chop factor

A new motive for the 'break-out' manager has emerged in the early 1990s and is encapsulated by the following domestic scene:

A highly successful 45-year-old, Joe Starr, is the MD of a company within a large group. He arrives home with some excellent news for his wife Ann.

"Hi, got some great news."
"Oh no, we're not moving again are we? We've only just settled here.'"
"No, no, this time we stay but I get to run the whole division. They have decided to retire Stan (his current boss) early and have given his job to me. Twenty per cent more cash, a sweet option deal and a new Mercedes S Class."
"That's great, well done. Let's go out and celebrate."

Later that evening, over a meal and champagne, Ann turns to Joe and says:

"Why did they retire Stan and how has he taken it?"
"Well, I guess they thought he had run out of steam and decided he should make way for a younger man – give me the chance to really prove myself."
"How old is Stan?"
"Fifty."
"Aha, so I guess that gives you five years max."

Joe is suddenly quiet. Joe then decides that she is right, and thinks:

"Ultimately, the only way I can control my destiny is by running my own business."

The second-time entrepreneur

The typical second-time entrepreneur involved in an MBI will:

– be in their late 40s or 50s,

- have been successful in a venture before (e.g. start-up, MBO) and will have sold out well,
- have £250,000 plus to invest (but this is not the greater part of their net worth),
- often invest and become an active three-day week chairman rather than a five- or six-day week operational CEO, and
- have a very good sense of timing; they probably sold their last company in 1987 or 1988.

Their motives are various. They may be bored or frustrated, or may have spent their first fortune and need to make some more capital. In the present lower interest rate environment, they may have experienced a dramatically lowered income (and such people rarely like using up capital). Or they may simply want to prove that they were not lucky the first time!

There are two main pitfalls associated with second-time entrepreneurs:

- that they were lucky the first time, and
- if they are returning following an extended holiday period, they may have lost some drive or sharpness.

From an investor's perspective, clearly the second-time entrepreneur or venturer, as they are sometimes known, is the easiest type of buy-in manager to deal with. Having done a deal of this type before, they know the rules of the game, are proficient at dealing with advisers and can empathise more easily with vendors. There are also increasing numbers given the volume of successful MBO exits.

Classic second-time MBI
Robert Wright is a classic example of a second-time MBI. Having spent 10 years as a pilot with BEA, he set up his own airline – Connectair – in 1984 with backing from 3i. The company grew steadily over the years, and in 1988 he was made an irresistible offer from Air Europe to sell out for £6.2 million. Three years later, when Air Europe crashed, he put together a plan to acquire Connectair's old licences to Antwerp, Rotterdam and Guernsey. 3i backed him again, and CityFlyer was born. Nearly three years on, Wright's new airline is making good profits on annual sales of around £20 million.

What sort of companies make good targets?

An analysis of 3i's portfolio of MBIs, illustrated in Exhibits 2, 3 and 4, provides a firm basis for assessing the nature of companies that tend to become MBI targets.

Ownership
Family companies. Very few families are able to repeat the Sainsbury example, and most bank managers know a family that held on too long. The reason that most family companies are attracted to an MBI manager is that such a manager will help to solve a succession problem, and this explains the match between the pie charts in Exhibits 2 and 3.

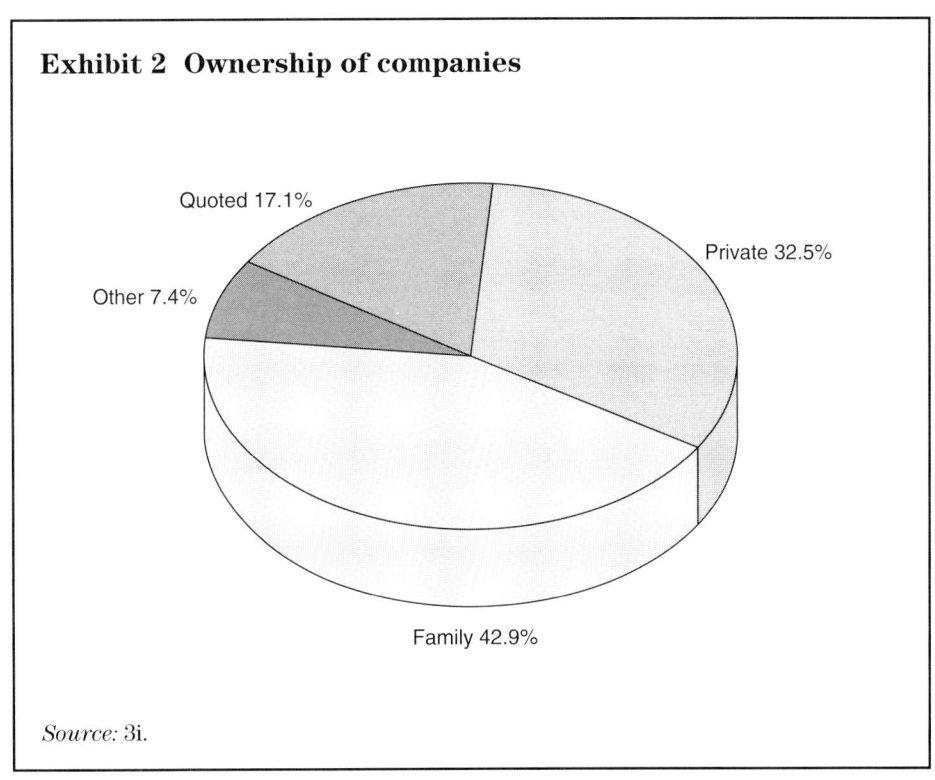

Exhibit 2 Ownership of companies

Quoted 17.1%

Private 32.5%

Other 7.4%

Family 42.9%

Source: 3i.

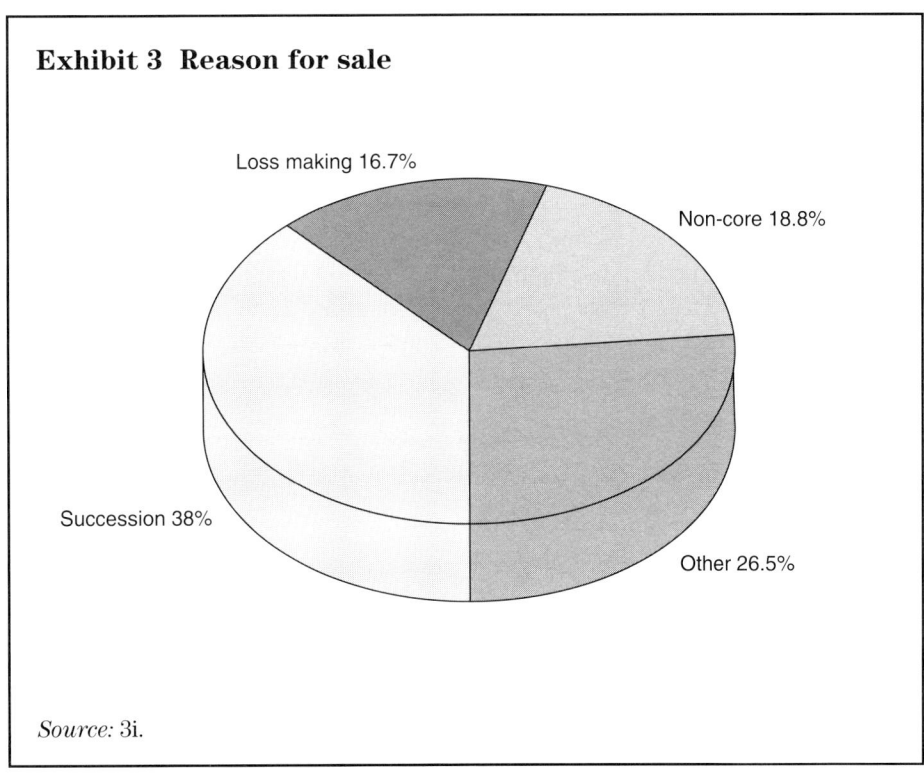

Exhibit 3 Reason for sale

Loss making 16.7%

Non-core 18.8%

Succession 38%

Other 26.5%

Source: 3i.

An MBI at a family company can retain the independence of the business, preserve its name and ensure greater continuity for employees. Families often have a preference for dealing with individuals rather than corporates. This is due to nervousness about what synergy really means if the alternative is a trade sale.

Family companies are also attracted to MBIs when the company has done well but, perhaps, is not as aggressively marketed as it could be and is capable of significant development. Most successful MBIs are successful through growth, rather than through cost reduction strategies.

Plc divestments. This is the ubiquitous 'non-core' disposal. The company may be a neglected jewel within the group – perhaps because it is very small by comparison to the other subsidiaries. The attraction of such divestments historically was that often money had been spent on the business, and it was at the point of turnaround that the group lost patience and sold. More care is needed now, as many such companies have been starved of development cash. It should also be noted that the reason given by groups for selling is almost always that the business is 'non-core' – even when this is not so!

Private. This class of company is the owner/manager business of reasonable scale. The following key issues should be addressed:

– Do you believe that the company is fairly represented by its accounts?
– How will the departure of the vendor affect the business? Is there sufficient second tier management?
– The super-profitable business in this category is often superficially the most attractive. The MBI manager has to remember that if it is being bought for a fair price, he or she has to make it grow. Is this possible?
– Due diligence on the part of the vendor is often lacking.

Sector

It is no great surprise that the bulk of MBIs backed to date have been businesses engaged in manufacturing, distribution and general industry (Exhibit 4). MBIs in service, retail and leisure are inherently more difficult to acquire as 'people businesses' suffer much more from loss of momentum during the sale process. They also have fewer assets, making financing more difficult. However, in practice these have been subsidiary difficulties to the main practical problem: historically, vendors of service businesses have simply wanted too much cash. Although this problem has lessened slightly in the early 1990s, it still exists and with service companies returning to growth, vendors are remembering the prices offered in the late 1980s.

Scale

The bulk of MBIs are businesses which turn over less than £10 million. A look at the nature of the ownership (Exhibit 2) reveals why. It is important for the MBI manager to avoid two key pitfalls in relation to the size of the company. Firstly, they must avoid the 'hamster wheel'. This occurs where a manager buys a

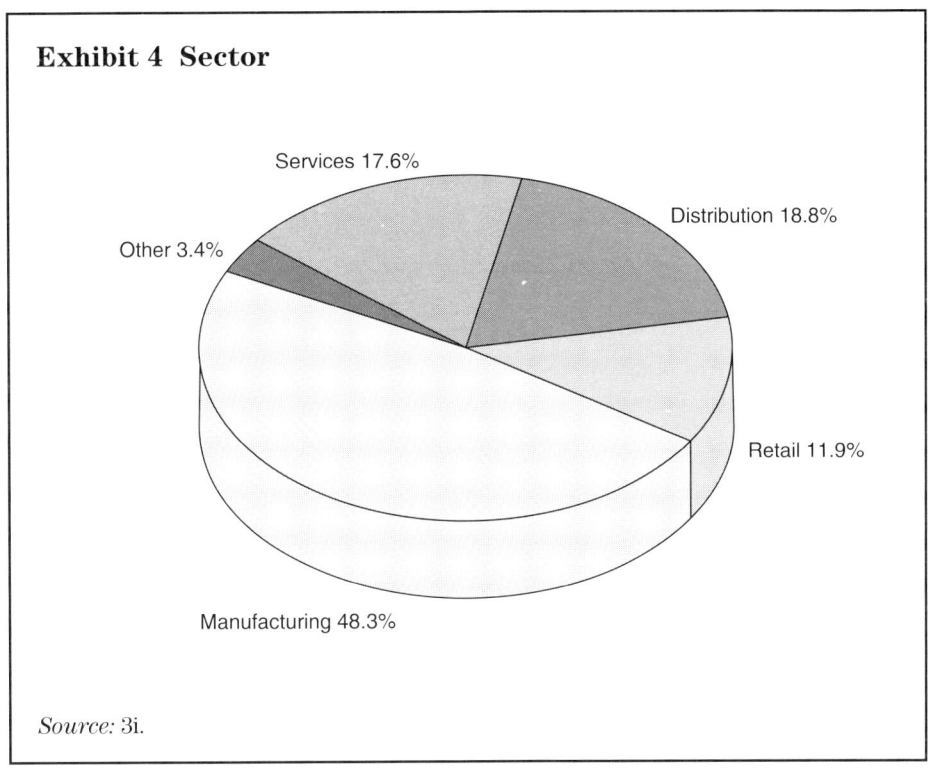

Exhibit 4 Sector

Services 17.6%

Distribution 18.8%

Other 3.4%

Retail 11.9%

Manufacturing 48.3%

Source: 3i.

company that is too small. Often these companies have few internal resources; the manager ends up doing everything himself and has no time left for development.

The second point to watch for is that many people from larger corporates feel very uncomfortable in the sub-£20 million turnover businesses which comprise most of the MBI targets. The very nature of the managing director's job is different, the people in the business are quite different and the nature of the day-to-day issues can be a shock to the 'multinational MD'.

Quoted targets

To date there have been few examples of plc MBIs – Cray Electronics is perhaps the most notable success. In the early 1990s, however, probably due to illiquidity at the lower end of the market, a small number of transactions took place.

A good example is the acquisition of Continuous Stationery plc. A small quoted company, it had grown quickly in the 1980s, mainly through acquisition. The recession, however, seriously stunted its growth and by the early 1990s it had two main operating subsidiaries – Prontaprint and Carwin Continuous.

It became obvious to the existing management that they were not progressing as a quoted company and in 1992 plans were launched to take the company private. 3i introduced Richard Raworth as an investing chairman and, together with managers from Prontaprint and Carwin, the £12 million deal was struck.

Key factors in success

3i has analysed its own MBI portfolio to reveal the following key factors for a successful MBI.

MD experience
Very few MBIs have worked where the MBI leader had not achieved significant managing director experience – typically five years and with full profit and loss and cash responsibility. It is far more important to have high quality MD experience than sector knowledge but clearly the combination of the two is even more powerful. Good MDs have the ability to pick and lead people, a vital skill in an MBI. They also have a good sense of what something is worth and an understanding of what customers want.

Knowledge of the individuals
3i points out that it has been far more successful when it has backed people it knows well and for some years it has had its own MBI Programme, whereby managers go through interviews, are referenced and then work with 3i on targeting and making approaches. Through helping them in this way 3i are able to obtain a much clearer view of their capabilities before it provides financing.

Financial structures
Pricing. Historically, successful MBI managers, on average, paid between 25 to 30 per cent less in terms of price, earnings and goodwill than their less successful counterparts. Prices have risen significantly since 1993 with average PEs moving from 4/5 to 8/9. This is a less startling move than it might first seem as the lower PEs would have been calculated on historical profits in a falling rather than a rising trend as was the case in 1993.

Gearing. It is also interesting to note that successful MBI managers take a more conservative approach to leverage. There is no meaningful average for gearing in this context, but typically successful MBI managers go for interest cover (PBIT/interest) of 2.5 to 3 and plan to keep their overdraft facility as a contingency by the end of the first year.

Deferred consideration. Only about a third of MBIs appear to contain an element of deferred consideration. This is surprising when one considers the risks involved. There is a school of thought which says that it is better to pay slightly more (a few per cent) and have a greater element deferred. Persuading vendors of private companies to sell with profit ratchets is inevitably difficult when they may not be involved in running the business. A simple scheme, subject only to warranties and indemnities, has therefore proved the most popular.

Don't buy in 1989. This is vitally important: buying at the top of the economic cycle presents a unique problem. Inevitably a highly priced transaction at the top of the cycle carries greater leverage and the prospect of the steepest decline in earnings.

Turnarounds. Contrary to the popular image, most MBIs are not turnarounds. It is significant that whereas the vast majority of MBI managers have turnaround experience, only a small minority want to invest the greater part of their net worth in one. Perhaps this is because only one in three will work! Institutions will tend to follow the principle adopted by 3i who will only back a turnaround MBI if the manager has achieved at least one successful turnaround before – as a managing director.

The 'Fits'

The effectiveness pressure curve (Exhibit 5) is a tool that 3i use in assessing the fit between the manager and the situation.

Psychologists believe that there is a clear relationship between how effective people are and the pressure that they are under. Simply put: no pressure, no work. Alternatively, if people are given targets and put under pressure, they become very effective. However, overload them and their performance deteriorates again.

In the context of an MBI, the greatest sources of pressure are where changes are taking place. These could be:

- doing an MBI in the first place,
- moving house,
- buying in a different sector,
- attempting to turnaround a company,
- a different scale of business,
- dealing with a different type of person, and
- personal borrowings.

The message is obvious: the manager who takes on too many tasks that are high pressure is asking for trouble. It is surprising, then, that many potential MBI managers are relaxed about taking on a business in a different sector, in a different place and on a different scale than they are used to – as well as attempting to turn the business around.

BIMBOs – Why so good?

The hybrid MBI/MBO (or BIMBO), which combines the objectivity of the MBI manager with the continuity of people within the business, often has significant advantages over a pure MBI:

More reliable information. The MBI manager is usually much better informed about the business than in a conventional deal. People within the business will respond to the manager's positive action in involving them in the equity. If they are signing up to the business plan, it is usually more reliable.

Less acquisitional drift. Usually, when a company is going through the sale process it suffers loss of momentum. The good managers are out looking for jobs – just in case – and the vendors are dreaming of the cash that is about to arrive. An

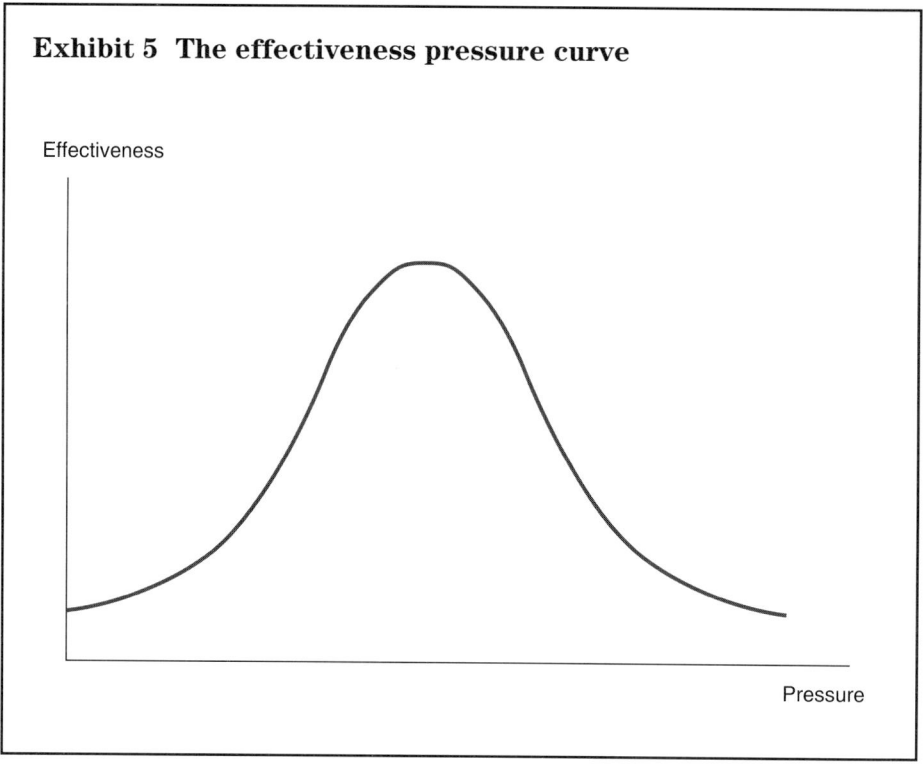

Exhibit 5 The effectiveness pressure curve

Effectiveness

Pressure

inordinate amount of time is spent showing people around, assisting due diligence, preparing information and in adviser meetings. No one is out selling and the business therefore suffers.

In MBOs this is known to occur to a much lesser degree because the people within the business have a strong incentive to make sure that the business is in the best shape possible. A BIMBO also goes a long way to achieving this.

Better motivation. The equity that incumbent management receives will provide greater motivation. The discussions over who gets what percentage and during the agreement of the business plan usually result in a tightly knit team. In a conventional MBI there is inevitably a sensitive 'getting to know you' time.

Competitive edge. A BIMBO sends a clear signal to a vendor about the MBI manager's approach. If the vendor is particularly concerned about what will happen to employees, this can be received very positively.

Of course, the main danger inherent in a BIMBO is that the wrong people will be invited to join in the equity. Untangling this type of mistake can be difficult. BIMBOs emerged as a result of MBI managers involving people who were within the business in the equity. Now 50 per cent of MBIs have this element present. However, recently several MBO transactions have turned into BIMBOs when a strong chairman or CEO has joined the MBO team.

One example is the purchase of The Benjamin Priest Group from its US parent, International Marine. Comprising 12 engineering components businesses, more than 50 managers invested in this buy-in/buy-out; the buy-in element came from Richard Miles, who was introduced from 3i's MBI Programme .

Conclusion

There is no doubt that MBIs have become a major feature of the business scene, playing a key role in the growth of corporate restructuring in the medium-sized business sector. In the UK, MBIs are now a well-established method of transferring the ownership of companies; the European market, although less developed, is growing quite quickly.

The individuals that lead buy-ins have an exceptional mix of personality and motivation. They have the drive and the enthusiasm to succeed and the confidence to leave their comfortable corporate jobs and to run independent businesses. Although they are risky transactions, MBIs can be very rewarding for both managers and their backers. There is no shortage of high calibre managers looking to buy into companies.

In addition, by taking the BIMBO route, much of the risk can be mitigated. Taking all these factors into consideration, the MBI phenomenon should continue to grow successfully in future years.

11

Larger management buy-outs

A larger management buy-out (or LMBO) in the UK may be defined as a buy-out or buy-in which involves a total funding of more than £10 million. Transactions of this size tend to have features which set them apart from the more numerous, smaller buy-outs, as we shall review in this chapter. They are often compared with the leveraged buy-outs (LBO) which originated in the United States, but in practice they may be distinguished from the LBO in the following ways:

– the LMBO is management-led rather than investor-driven,
– the LMBO is less highly leveraged with the very high gearing of the LBO reflecting, at least historically, a more relaxed US attitude to cash flow lending coupled with the availability of 'junk' bond finance,
– the source of the majority of LMBOs has been a sale from a parent company, whereas the majority of LBOs have involved the purchase of a quoted public company, taking advantage of alleged undervaluation by the market place, and
– the LMBO is rarely predicated on substantial sales of assets or a total break-up of the target entity, whereas this is often the case with the LBO.

History of the LMBO market

Between 1 January 1984 and 30 June 1994 a total of 463 LMBOs were completed. Exhibit 1 shows the annual numbers of such deals analysed according to different size bands.

It was the 1981–83 recession, coupled with the financial assistance relaxations in the Companies Act 1981, which created the early opportunities for managers to buy-out their businesses at attractive prices; the vendors were receivers and parent companies keen to improve liquidity in the face of pressure from their banks. However, at that time unquoted equity from institutional investors was in short supply and this, together with a conservative asset based approach to debt financing by UK clearing banks, meant that a £10 million transaction was considered large. During the past 10 years the picture has changed dramatically and the growth in the venture capital market during the 1980s has resulted in a current membership of the British Venture Capital Association (BVCA) of over 100. The vast majority of these claim the capability of arranging an LMBO, although Exhibit 2 shows that there are currently only about 15 consistent players in the market.

Exhibit 1 Number of larger management buy outs 1984–94 (first six months) by size

	84	85	86	87	88	89	90	91	92	93	94
10m to 25m	4	17	14	13	24	38	40	22	27	26	22
25m to 50m	2	–	7	6	12	16	12	10	14	16	10
50m to 100m	1	5	4	6	9	10	4	5	8	5	4
100m to 250m	–	–	2	6	5	5	3	7	4	3	1
250m +	–	1	–	2	5	3	1	–	1	1	–
Total	7	23	27	33	55	72	60	44	54	51	37

Source: KPMG Peat Marwick.

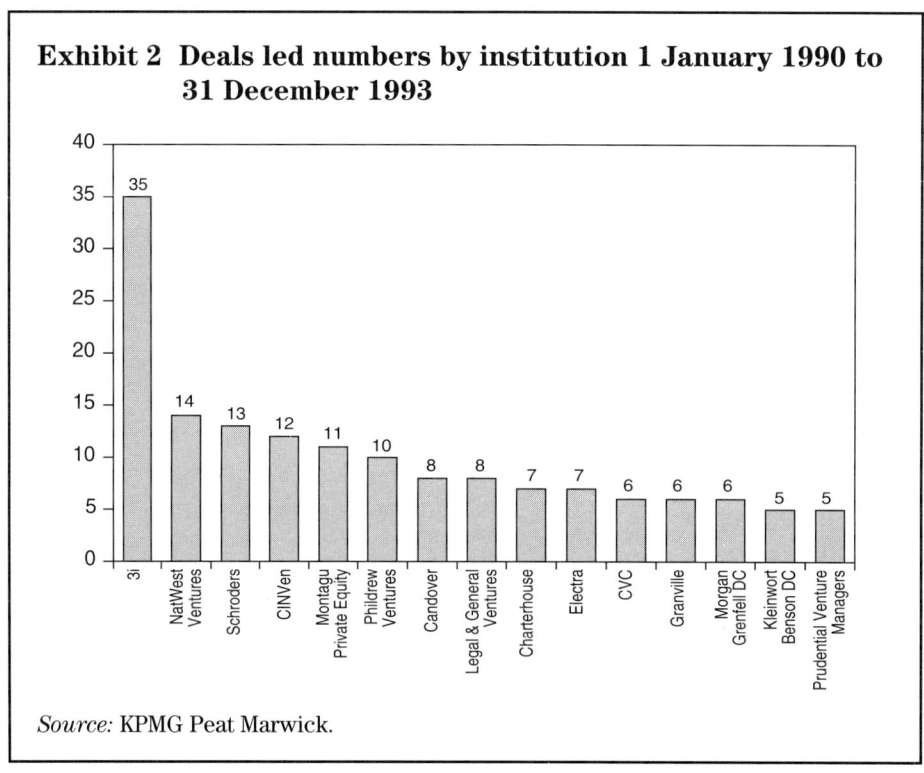

Exhibit 2 Deals led numbers by institution 1 January 1990 to 31 December 1993

Source: KPMG Peat Marwick.

However, these rather simplistic analyses mask a significant number of trends which have developed since the LMBO first became popular in the early 1980s – some of them short-lived and others more permanent. Syndication and fund raising have become inextricably linked to an increasing desire, even need, to lead transactions; the availability of debt and what constitutes an acceptable level of gearing has fluctuated considerably. This has had a major impact on the numbers and size of deals completed; and the public-to-private transaction was born (and, many would say, has virtually died).

Types of LMBO

There are a number of different ways in which deals can be analysed.

Deal size

We have already seen, in Exhibit 1, an analysis by deal size. This shows an overall growth in the market during the period to 1989 with a fall-off in numbers since then. Within these figures we can see that deals greater than £50 million, which were virtually non-existent in the early years, grew to a peak of 19 in 1988, fell back sharply two years later and revived somewhat to a total of 13 in 1992, only to fall again in 1993. It is noticeable that 1988 and 1989 together saw eight of the overall total of 14 deals worth £250 million or more, whereas only two were completed in the period 1991–93. Most people would attribute this change to a more sombre view of the growth prospects of the largest companies and, in particular, the sharp change in acceptable gearing levels, which is discussed later.

By contrast, in the price range £10–£50 million, the numbers peaked in the years 1989 and 1990 and, although they have fallen back, 1992 and 1993 each exceeded a healthy 40 deals completed. If this category of deal shows the true health of the LMBO market, as many commentators suggest, then the patient is not as fit as in the late 1980s but is, nonetheless, in reasonably good health.

It is also interesting to note that the most recent statistics suggest that the patient is now fully recovered with 37 deals completed in the first six months of 1994, including a total of 32 in the £10–£50 million price range.

Nature of Vendor

In terms of pointers for the future, one of the most interesting ways of analysing deals is by vendor type. This is illustrated in Exhibit 3 and there are a number of features worth highlighting.

The LMBO is now widely accepted by companies and their financial advisers as a viable alternative to finding trade buyers for their non-core subsidiaries. As a result, UK and foreign vendors have been the source of 78 per cent (by number) of all LMBOs completed in the UK in the period under consideration.

As corporate vendors play such a prominent role in the overall LMBO market, it is easy to conclude that the health of the market will track that of the overall corporate finance market. As the corporate appetite for acquisitions increases this is likely to throw off unwanted subsidiaries and divisions which, in theory, can boost the number of opportunities available for future LMBOs.

**Exhibit 3 Analysis of UK MBOs by vendor 1 January 1984–
30 June 1994**

	Number	(%)	By value
UK listed parent	210	45	49
Private	93	20	8
Overseas parent	62	13	12
MBO of listed company	32	7	22
Privatisation	31	7	5
Receivership	27	6	3
Previous MBO	8	2	1
Total	463	100	100

Source: KPMG Peat Marwick.

However, we must also remember that an increased acquisition appetite means more competition for the LMBO buyer than was the case in years of depressed corporate activity such as 1992. Indeed it was often the case in that year that institutional funders supporting an LMBO were the only cash buyers available to an often distressed vendor – an ironic twist on the adage, often applied to MBOs, that 'cash is king'. It is difficult to predict whether or not LMBO funders will, in the future, be prepared to compete with corporate buyers, who can now pay for acquisitions with very highly rated paper. Does the increase in LMBOs during the first half of 1994 suggest that MBO specialists are paying too much or is the combination of more available bank funding and increased confidence in the UK economy leading to more aggressive but nonetheless sensible pricing? Only time will tell.

Privatisations and receiverships, although relatively small in number, were a particular feature of the 1992 figures with port privatisations and buy-outs from the receiver – the ultimate 'distressed' vendor – considerably boosting the figures for that year. In 1993 we witnessed a slightly quieter year with the absence of such deals and the virtual disappearance of the pub deal. However, 1994 emerged with strong figures for the first half despite the fact that the next wave of privatisations – the London bus companies and British Rail – have only begun to feature since July 1994.

The final major category of vendor type is the LMBO of a public company. A total of 32 of these have been completed to date and are of sufficient interest to a warrant a separate section within this chapter although it seems as if this source of deals has all but disappeared.

Regionalisation

One other pattern worth discussing is that of regionalisation.

Exhibit 4 shows a regional analysis of deals (by number and value) comparing figures for the period 1 January 1981 to 31 December 1988 with those from 1 January 1984 – 30 June 1993. The most striking change is the drop from 55 per cent of all deals in the South East of England to 47 per cent with the 'missing' 8 per cent largely being captured by the North Western region. The South East still enjoys a higher percentage of LMBOs by number than its 36 per cent share of GDP would suggest, principally due to the number of head offices located there. We have, however, seen a steady growth in the opportunities outside the South East as funding becomes less London orientated and, in particular, the professional communities in the regions become more experienced in this type of transaction. This shift is strongly reflected in 3i's own penetration of the LMBO market with six out of the 11 deals which we led in 1992 located outside the South East and all nine in 1993 similarly regionally located.

Exhibit 4 Analysis of deals by region

| | 1 Jan 1981–31 Dec 1988 | | 1 Jan 1984–30 June 1993 | |
	Number (%)	Value (%)	Number (%)	Value (%)
South East (excluding London)	31	36	29	43
London	24	31	18	20
West Midlanes	8	3	9	5
Yorks & Humberside	11	6	10	9
South West	5	8	5	6
East Midlands	6	3	5	3
North West	5	2	10	6
North	2	3	2	1
Scotland	5	3	6	4
Wales	2	3	2	1
East Anglia	1	1	3	1
N. Ireland	0	0	1	1

Source: KPMG Peat Marwick.

Future trends

What, therefore, will be the picture in the mid and later 1990s for the type of deal available? Contrary to many people's predictions, 1994 has seen a surge in numbers with 37 deals completed in the first six months despite the absence of privatisations. Clearly the full year will show an increased total over 1993 with the probability that we will see in excess of 60 deals – the second best year ever recorded.

The corporate vendor will continue to be the major provider of deals to our market although the stock of privatisations could be, albeit temporarily, replenished. As the economy grows stronger receiverships are likely to diminish as a source of deals and the public-to-private transaction will continue to 'provide little trouble for the scorer'. We may well see more LMBOs of previous buy-out companies with lower interest rates than during the 1980s and the increased desire of institutional funders in some of the earlier deals to engineer an exit. Nonetheless taken over the long term there seems to be a base of 50–60 deals per annum, the vast majority in the £10–£50 million size range (and many located outside London and the South East), which will continue to be completed in what is now a well-established market.

LMBOS of a listed company

There have been 32 LMBOs of listed companies ('public-to-privates') during the 13 year period under review. However, as Exhibit 5 shows, 26 of these were completed in the four-year period 1987–90. It is even more astonishing to note that 35 per cent of the total value of all LMBOs in that period comprised public-to-privates with the figure in 1989 being 65 per cent!

Why, then, were they so popular during that short period, and why has that popularity waned?

Exhibit 5 Comparison of listed and unlisted MBOs over £10m

	Number			Value (£m)		
	Total	*Listed*	*(%)*	*Total*	*Listed*	*(%)*
1984	25	–	–	860	–	–
1985	23	2	9	870	70	8
1986	27	2	7	940	35	4
1987	33	4	12	2,750	486	18
1988	55	6	11	4,510	940	21
1989	72	12	17	5,850	3,802	65
1990	60	4	7	2,050	167	8
1991	44	1	2	1,880	17	1
1992	54	1	2	2,310	12	1
1993	51	–	–	2,000	–	–
Total	444	32	7	24,020	5,529	23

Source: KPMG Peat Marwick.

Many of the public-to-private deals have become household names – sometimes for the wrong reasons, e.g. Isosceles and Magnet. Ironically it was the latter which prompted a significant tightening by the Takeover Panel of the rules and regulations governing an attempt by existing management to purchase their employer and take the company private. The very early indication of interest by a management team that is now required by the Takeover Panel rules, together with the provision of all information to other potential bidders, has naturally made management teams very wary of putting their employer 'into play'.

Institutions have also learnt some lessons from their late 1980s experience in public-to-private transactions – particularly the need to perform full due diligence on the target company in order to satisfy themselves that this is a worthwhile home for their cash. This requirement alone is likely to severely limit the numbers of public companies which potentially lend themselves to the LMBO route.

The supply is further limited by the obvious drawbacks arising from there being no single vendor and the uncertainties this creates. Even where there is a sizeable single shareholder (say 40 per cent plus) many uncertainties remain; not the least of these is the need to gain acceptances from the holders of 90 per cent of the shares before the company can be taken private and the senior debt providers granted the expected security over the assets.

The delays and uncertainties outlined above mean that either substantial contingent fees expended by professionals can mount up or that institutions need to underwrite a significant fee budget with a low probability that the deal will go ahead – particularly if the deal concerns a large company which may be attractive to a number of potential buyers.

This, of itself, should not prevent public-to-privates taking place provided institutional returns are higher than normal to compensate for the additional risks taken. However this has not been the case historically. Indeed Exhibit 6 shows that of the various categories of deal for which KPMG gather information the public-to-private is by far the worst in terms of return with internal rates of return of minus 36 per cent.

Exhibit 6 Analysis of LMBOs by vendor. Exited by end September 1993

	Number of deals	IRR(%)
Government	14	80
UK unlisted companies	24	59
UK listed companies	66	57
Overseas companies	21	63
Public (listed MBOs)	11	–36

Source: KPMG Peat Marwick.

All these difficulties and the poor returns suggest that in future the public-to-private LMBO will be the exception rather than the rule. The typical profile of future public-to-private deals is likely to include most of the following features:

– a relatively small company which is not particularly attractive to a range of trade purchasers,
– a significant block of shares held in one or a small number of hands,
– a situation in which the shares are thinly traded, so that the LMBO offers the only real opportunity for existing shareholders to obtain a fair price for their investment,
– a situation in which the institutional investors in the LMBO are given sufficient access to perform a proper due diligence exercise,

– a situation in which the new institutional investors are bringing something additional to the table such as a highly rated new Chairman or Chief Executive, and

– offers of participation in the LMBO to those existing shareholders who are willing to roll over their investment.

The features outlined above describe the background to one of only two public-to-private deals completed since 1990 – Continuous Stationery plc (the Prontaprint franchise company). A common view in the industry is that future public-to-privates will be small in number and much more likely to have a profile similar to Prontaprint than Magnet or Isosceles.

Structures

One of the key aspects of the LMBO market has been the significant fluctuations in structures which have been acceptable over the years. The two main types of debt funding are considered below; the equity side of the funding equation is described separately in a later section entitled 'Syndication and fund raising'.

Senior debt

In many ways the availability of senior debt and the attitude of lenders have been the biggest influences in the LMBO market.

In the early 1980s, the size of an LMBO was largely dictated by the ability to fund the transaction both in terms of debt capacity as well as equity. Initially the UK clearing banks were cautious about lending to this sector without substantial asset coverage. However, the success of early LMBOs, together with the arrival of foreign competition, encouraged the clearers to become more involved and to give greater emphasis to the merits of cash flow lending. Their strong showing in the table of recent debt leaders (Exhibit 7) suggests that they have learnt very quickly.

Exhibit 7 Leading debt arrangers 1990–93

	Total number
Bank of Scotland	70
NatWest	34
Barclays/BZW	23
Midland/Samuel Montagu	20
Royal Bank of Scotland	9
Morgan Grenfell	5

Source: KPMG Peat Marwick.

However, the rapid growth in the number and size of larger MBOs could not have been achieved without the presence of foreign banks – particularly

Continental and Japanese institutions. Their enthusiasm for participating in this sector not only reduced the debt underwriter's risk by providing 'sell down' capacity but also enabled the amount of senior debt on offer to be increased. The increasing buoyancy of the debt market impacted margins which gradually declined from around 2 per cent to as low as 1.25 per cent in 1989 – despite the fact that average gearing levels had risen to almost 6:1 (Exhibit 8).

There was then a significant change with gearing falling dramatically to a trough of 1.1:1 in the second half of 1992 while at the same time margins widened from 2 per cent to 2.5 per cent and fees increased commensurately. The reasons for this dramatic shift were, as with all markets, directly related to supply and demand.

The change since 1989 occurred because of the withdrawal of many US, Continental and Japanese banks from the UK LMBO market. The most obvious reason for this withdrawal was the poor performance of the UK economy, with high interest rates causing problems for highly geared structures both in terms of interest costs and depressed consumer demand. A number of other factors on the international scene also contributed to the scarcity of willing debt providers; those factors included the Gulf War, the US and European recessions and the changes in banking capital adequacy rules which was exacerbated by falling asset values impacting the banks' equity base.

Exhibit 8 Analysis of gearing of UK LMBOs

Period	Total funding (£m)	Equity (£m)	Mezzanine (£m)	Debt (£m)	Gearing (E:M+D)
4 years to:					
December 1984	857	370	–	487	1.3
December 1985	9,069	2,538	706	5,825	2.6
6 months to:					
June 1989	1,705	430	158	1,117	3.0
December 1989	4,146	598	706	2,842	5.9
June 1990	1,273	288	153	832	3.4
December 1990	780	263	63	454	2.0
June 1991	700	324	30	346	1.2
December 1991	1,180	432	102	646	1.7
June 1992	1,045	419	62	564	1.5
December 1992	1,259	584	34	641	1.2
June 1993	1,005	447	51	507	1.2
December 1993	1,072	461	47	564	1.3

Source: KPMG Peat Marwick.

Although the figures suggest that there has been little change since 1992 this is far from the truth. There has been a significant increase in the number of banks who are willing to either lead or underwrite/participate in LMBO transactions and this increasing competition has already seen thinner margins and fees with 2 per cent over Libor becoming the norm and lower figures quoted for larger deals where competition is particularly intense. We have not yet seen a significant shift in structures although competition will, no doubt, have its effect in this area too. However, it is anybody's guess whether or not gearing and margins will revert towards the figures seen in 1989. In early 1993 virtually everyone would have predicted that too many banking and equity fingers had been burnt for that to happen – it is now likely that at least some commentators are less categoric on that particular point.

Mezzanine debt

Given the tentative approach by UK banks to cash flow lending in the early 1980s, it soon became apparent to deal originators that if the price expectations of vendors were to be satisfied, while continuing to offer attractive returns to the equity holders, then the UK needed to follow the US example and develop its own subordinated debt market.

The first MBOs involving sizeable mezzanine strips took place in 1985 with the Haden, Lawson Mardon and Caradon transactions; they were subscribed for in full by US institutions. These deals led UK institutions to accept more readily the idea that future cash flows in a stable business offered an alternative to 'bricks and mortar' and ' stocks and debtors' as a basis for lending. As a result, most of the leading mezzanine arrangers in the United Kingdom are of UK origin although the US institutions still feature quite strongly.

Exhibit 9 Leading mezzanine arrangers 1990–93

	Total number
3i	15
Intermediate Capital Group	10
NatWest Ventures/NatWest	8
Legal & General/Mithras	5
Chase Manhattan	3
First Brittania	3

Source: KPMG Peat Marwick.

The number of LMBOs using mezzanine increased from five in 1985 (22 per cent of the total for that year) to 38 in 1989 – representing around 54 per cent of that year's total. Since then we have seen a significant decline in the use of mezzanine (only 24 per cent of deals used mezzanine in 1993) as overall deal prices have fallen and the availability of equity funding has increased; another factor is that most equity providers are now keen to reduce the number of funding parties involved. Therefore, despite the decrease in availability of senior debt and the resultant drop in gearing, equity providers have provided significantly larger amounts of equity in LMBOs foregoing high headline IRRs in return for a greater degree of stability. This has eliminated the provision of mezzanine funding by a separate provider of funds (i.e. not the same player or players who have provided the equity) to all but the largest transactions – usually deals of £30–£40 million plus and I believe that this deal size will be the focus for most separately provided mezzanine in the future.

One final feature of the mezzanine debate has been the increased use of 'vendor stakes'. These were particularly prevalent in 1988, when prices where high, and again in 1990 and 1991 (Exhibit 10) when prices required by vendors often failed to reflect the continual drop in underlying profits of the target company. As vendor stakes were often denominated in subordinated loans or preference shares with longer repayment dates, low yields and limited rights, they could be introduced as a means of bridging any gap between the pricing expectations of vendor and purchasers. As we are often likely to see such a mismatch it seems fair to conclude that the vendor stake has become a permanent feature of the LMBO funding market.

Exhibit 10 Analysis of UK LMBOs with vendor stakes

	LMBOs with vendor stakes	Total LMBOs (excl. listed)	With vendor stakes (%)
1981–85	3	45	7
1986	2	25	8
1987	5	29	17
1988	14	49	29
1989	11	59	19
1990	17	54	31
1991	16	43	37
1992	13	53	25
1993	11	51	22
Total	92	408	195

Source: KPMG Peat Marwick.

Syndication and fund raising

In the early part of the 1980s the size of deal completed was constrained not only by the availability of senior debt but by the amount of equity funding which could be sourced for any single transaction. As the number of players and their available funding was limited, pre-completion 'club' deals between like-minded institutions were put together which helped avoid any syndication risk but complicated the deal process considerably and resulted in a number of potential investment opportunities falling away prior to completion.

In order to overcome this problem, the concept of a transaction being underwritten by two or three institutions and then syndicated following completion was introduced in about 1984. At the same time the numbers of willing syndicatees (followers of other people's deals) began to grow; this gave the deal leaders and underwriters confidence that they could accept the risk of underwriting larger exposures as they knew they would be able to sell down to their desired level of exposure shortly after completion.

Despite the growth in numbers and in the investment capacity of equity providers, syndicates in the mid-1980s were still very large with 83 per cent of all MBOs (by value) having syndicates of more than 4 members. Indeed the LMBO of Westbury, an £18m deal completed in 1984, had an equity syndicate of 17! By 1991 the figure for syndicates of more than four members had dropped to 23 per cent (Exhibit 11), and since then the number of syndicatees has continued to diminish. What are the reasons behind this dramatic change in market practice?

In order to answer this question, we must study individually the reasons why any institution wishes to syndicate a deal. One major reason is to attempt to spread the deal leader/underwriter's risk. However, as the cash available to some of the larger LMBOs practitioners grew (Exhibit 12) they had less need to sell down from their initial position in order to spread their risk.

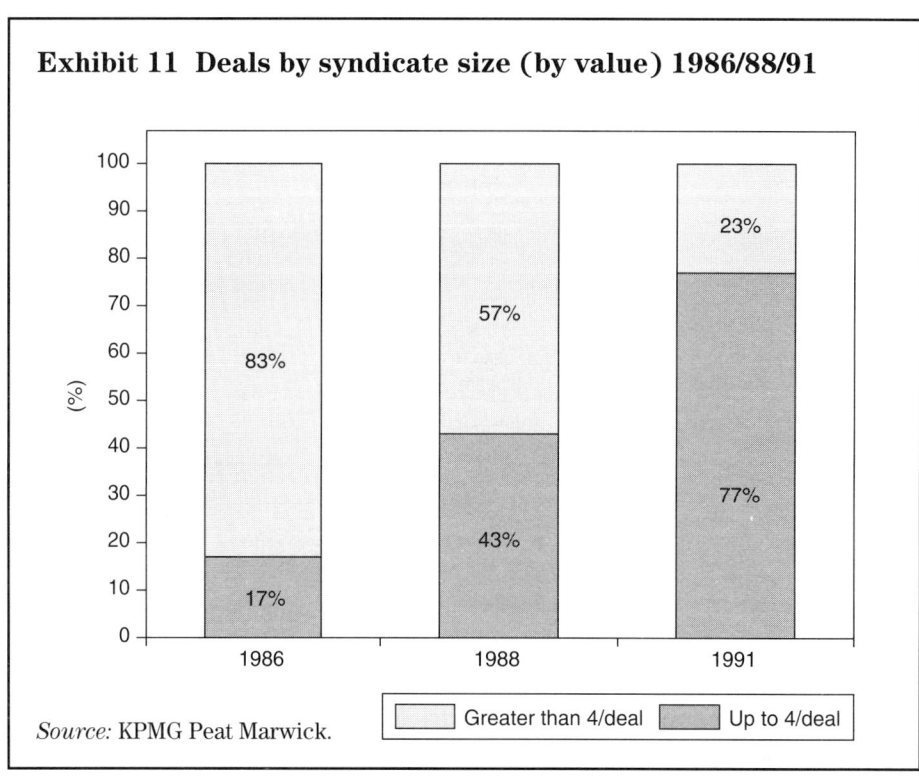

Exhibit 11 Deals by syndicate size (by value) 1986/88/91

Source: KPMG Peat Marwick.

Greater than 4/deal   Up to 4/deal

Probably the most common reason for syndication is the desire of the deal leader to avoid acquiring a controlling position in the target. However, as the number of specialist funds in the market grew, the legal mechanism used to attract their funding allowed them to avoid having legal control of the target in any single legal entity – even where the funds under their management held 90 per cent of the ordinary shares!

A third reason for syndication is reciprocity. This remains a relevant factor in the smaller syndications market which now exists but it is increasingly outweighed by the demands of funds providers – the ultimate judge of whether many existing fund managers actually retain the ability to write any new business – who wish to see the fund managers add value by leading and managing investments, rather than swapping shares in syndicates with each other. Fund raising is clearly the most significant factor influencing the future of the whole venture capital market and, in particular, the LMBO segment of that market; fund managers are therefore increasingly sensitive to the demands of the major investing institutions.

Exhibit 12 reveals that before the record achievement of 1994 when over £2 billion of funds are known to have been raised the period 1988–90 represented a peak for fund raising. This was often done on the back of a limited track record as far as leading or originating transactions was concerned. Now that the industry is more mature and there are more players to choose from, the fund provider is better able to make an informed choice about which fund to support.

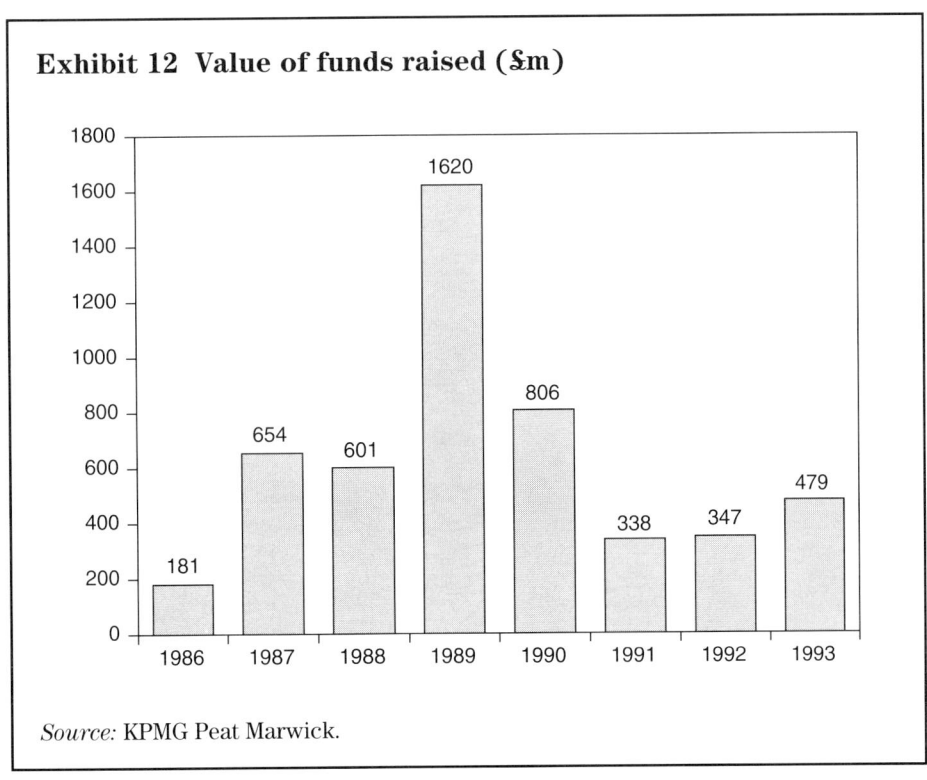

Exhibit 12 Value of funds raised (£m)

Source: KPMG Peat Marwick.

At the same time as track records have built up the UK economy went into recession; the extraordinary returns available on many deals completed in the early and mid-1980s averaged out to a more modest level when set alongside some of the highly priced underperforming deals completed later in the decade. The very illiquid unquoted investment asset therefore became a less obvious and less attractive area for an allocation of funds within a pension fund's or investment manager's portfolio. These difficulties were evidenced by figures for 1991 to 1993 where relatively modest figures of £300–£450 million were raised in each of these years.

However, increasing confidence in the UK economy, together with the increase in returns from the rising number of exits with attractive IRR's, has given a significant boost to fund raising and a large number of institutions returned to the fund raising market in 1994, raising a record amount of over £2 billion.

Early in 1993 the availability of funds was seen as the key issue for the industry. Indeed it was estimated at that stage that anything up to 40 existing BVCA members were trying to raise new funds. Although on the face of it £2 billion funds raised seems like a success for the industry, the reality is that this money has been concentrated into the hands of a relatively small number of successful funds. Why did this concentration come about?

The providers of funds now have a much clearer individual track record upon which to base their decisions than they did first time around in the mid/late 1980s. They have also learnt a number of important lessons, not least the impact which fees and carried interests can have on their returns and the fact that the very high returns promised in many of the original fund raising documents have rarely, if ever, been delivered. This, together with the much sharper focus on the returns made on deals led rather than those followed has led to a much more selective approach by fund providers both in terms of amounts invested and numbers of funds supported.

Thus at least some of the 40 would-be fund raisers have failed to raise new funding and will therefore find it difficult or impossible to make new investments. Although they may be able to continue to manage existing investments within their current funds, it seems likely that Jon Moulton's prediction, when he was at Schroder Ventures, that '1991 will be a year where the industry becomes mature, i.e. shrunken and shrivelled' is belatedly going to come true.

Exits

So far we have concentrated on the 'front end' of the LMBO process, i.e. making the investment. It is, however, important to remember exits.

There are a number of differences between the LMBO and its smaller counterpart, the MBO. Some of the major ones arise out of the syndication of the various financing strips. That there are often more layers of finance included in the overall funding package; and the additional numbers of people, both professionals (accountants, lawyers, etc.) and institutional representatives that these factors bring to the transaction, make the process more complex.

However, one of the key differences is the perception that the LMBO changes ownership within a relatively short period of three to five years. The fact that exits are very important in crystallising the returns of many venture capitalists, particularly those who are fund raising, is a very pertinent factor. Also relevant is the fact that we are dealing with reasonably sized companies which are therefore likely to be attractive, at least in principle, to a range of trade purchasers – as well as being possible flotation candidates.

As a result of the above perceptions, many deals in the late 1980s were structured by equity houses and banks on the basis that they would float within three to four years. However, of the 424 deals completed as at 30 September 1993, only 150 had exited at that date and 21 of those businesses had gone into receivership. The number of deals not yet exited at that date – 274 – represents virtually five years of deals on a count back basis. Despite the strong exit performance during 1994 the number of deals where exits have not been achieved suggests that the present practice, of structuring deals so that they can reduce gearing to a more traditional level through trading alone, seems a sensible approach which should continue into the future.

The future

What, then, does the future hold for the LMBO market and its venture capital adherents? While 1994 may well produce figures comparable with those of 1989, in the longer term an increase in competition from trade buyers should lead to a consistent base of 50–60 deals per annum.

With the return of a range of banks to the senior debt market structures will become less conservative than in 1992 but will probably not revisit some of the ratios which we experienced in the late 1980s. This will mean that deals will tend to be structured to trade out of high initial gearing based on the more realistic assumption that the timing of exit cannot be planned with any great certainty.

The use of mezzanine debt will be more restricted than in 1989 when 54 per cent of deals were partly funded by this mechanism. Separate mezzanine strips provided by separate funders are likely to be limited to the larger deals (£30 million plus) although vendor financing is a feature which will, I believe, continue to play a sizeable role in the market.

However, the most important factor affecting the market will be equity funding. The somewhat smaller market together with the fall in syndications activity cannot support the number of participants now present. Fund providers have the information available to become more selective as to whom they will support and they may therefore commit fewer funds overall to what is seen as an illiquid market.

This rationalisation should not be seen as in any way a failure of the market. It is natural in any market to see a period of consolidation and fall-out following rapid early growth. There is little doubt that the LMBO market is here to stay. It is, nonetheless, ironic that 'cash is king', a core principle for all MBOs, has now become a very relevant factor for the survival and prosperity of many venture capitalist funders themselves.